THE INTIMATE RESISTANCE
A PHILOSOPHY OF PROXIMITY

Josep Maria Esquirol is a philosopher, essayist and professor of philosophy at the University of Barcelona. Winner of numerous prizes, he was awarded the *Premi Ciutat de Barcelona* in 2015 and the *Premio Nacional de Ensayo* in 2016. *The Intimate Resistance* has been translated into many different languages and this is the first time his work has appeared in the English Language.

Douglas Suttle is a teacher, translator and publisher from London. Among other Catalan writers, he has translated Jordi Llavina and Narcís Oller into English.

'The author's talent radiates in defining the context of said resistance. And by doing so not via abstract thought, but by painting us a picture with his own personal philosophical ingredients — ignoring dogmatisms — of the era we are now living in, in this opulent and privileged part of the planet.'
— Sergi Pàmies, author of *The Art of Wearing a Trench Coat*

'A beautiful reflection expressed through intimate words and a strange, profound proximity regarding the different things humans can do with their autonomy.'
— Robert Juan-Cantavella, *El Mundo*

'The very opposite of self-help, this is a life manual, full of questions and the reasoning of facts and the things that surround and affect us.'
— Francesc Serés

'Esquirol's recipe is proximity to the everyday, to the people closest to us, not to a specific day or temporality, but rather always and everywhere. Silence and reflection and great companions in resistance.'
— Lluís Foix, *La Vanguardia*

'Esquirol speaks to us of philosophy as a good life, and only in a Stoic sense. It is a wager, backed up by the philosophy of the other, of the you as a "teacher and doctor". It is to hear our own finitude.'
— Juan Malpartida, *ABC*

'Professor Esquirol writes in an entertaining, simple and very, very beautiful way. This is a compass, a fine book to enjoy again and again.'
— Manuel Astur

FUM D'ESTAMPA PRESS LTD.
LONDON — BARCELONA
WWW.FUMDESTAMPA.COM

This translation has been published in Great Britain
by Fum d'Estampa Press Limited 2021

001

La resistència íntima by Josep Maria Esquirol
Copyright © 2015 by Josep Maria Esquirol
© 2015 by Quaderns Crema, S.A. (Acantilado, Barcelona)
All rights reserved

Translation copyright © Douglas Suttle, 2021
With many thanks to Berta Sáenz Almazán for her help and remarkable patience.

The moral right of the author and translator has been asserted
Set in Minion Pro

Printed and bound by TJ Books Ltd, Padstow, Cornwall
A CIP catalogue record for this book is available from the British Library

ISBN: 978-1-913744-08-3

Series design by 'el mestre' Rai Benach

This work was translated with the help of a grant from the Institut Ramon Llull.

**institut
ramon llull**
Catalan Language and Culture

FUM D'ESTAMPA PRESS

THE INTIMATE RESISTANCE

A PHILOSOPHY OF PROXIMITY

JOSEP MARIA ESQUIROL

Translated by

DOUGLAS SUTTLE

CONTENTS

In Memory of Josep
And of Maria Teresa from cal Sabater coix

Moment

The plate on the table, the olive oil and bread. The table laid, the pot simmering, and the glasses half steamed up by the vapour rising from the stew. What removes this everyday image so far from the nihilistic experience? What of it fails to comply with scenes of the void and the absurd? What do we associate with it? Where does it take us? The warm plate on the table, full of something that is cooked — or was once cooked — *at home*. Nothing sybaritic; nothing sophisticated. More than anything, we associate it with the care for others that the act of cooking represents, company and the shelter of home. Also, of course, the pleasure of eating and our 'memory' of the constituent parts: the olive oil we drizzle over our food brings to mind the olive tree and the firm earth into which it sinks its roots; the bright sky overhead; the mature fruit; the harvest; the press. Bread, too, reminds us of the earth and the heavens, vast fields of wheat at the edge of the blue. Yet it also bears us away to something even more primordial: others. Bread is something to be shared, and our companions (*com* 'with, together' and *pān* 'bread') are, literally, those with whom we share it. Sitting around the table, our fellow diners both create and are community. The warm plate on the table conjures up images of Bartleby, Melville's literary hero and marginal personality who today is still evoked by t-shirts and other products bearing the unsettling phrase: 'I would prefer not to.' Bartleby never had a place at table. At least, based on rather overwhelming evidence, this was the suspicion of the lawyer who employed him. Nobody prepared and served Bartleby his lunch, not even an anonymous chef in some local restaurant. Nor did he ever break bread with anyone: he ate alone, hidden away in his office. So perhaps it is not totally surprising that Bartleby eventually died of voluntary starvation — well, his body died but his spirit flounders and fails as a result of something quite different.

We renew our lives together, and our delight in food and drink takes on a spiritual dimension as we sit together around the table, sharing words and gestures. Collective life depends on the act of eating together. It's precisely due to this that images of isolation — not solitude — are so unsettling. The bread and salt, the feast, grief and peace: community and living together, however difficult and uncertain, depends on sharing these things.

I. DISINTEGRATION AND RESISTANCE

There are unrivalled solitudes to be had in their sharing. In fact, only those capable of solitude can truly be around others. Painted on the wall of a hermit's bedroom in a run-down house in the Italian city of Turin, one can find these words: 'He who goes to the desert is not a deserter.' Paradoxically, despite the meaning of *deserter* (someone who runs away to an uninhabited place, forsakes or abandons a cause or person, people etc.) this inscription might well contain the whole truth. It is clear that, in a figurative sense, the desert is not only to be found in vast stretches of arid, featureless land or in seas of sand presided over by a punishing sun: the desert is everywhere and nowhere at once. Found, for instance, in the very hearts of cities. Those who venture into the desert are, first and foremost, those who *resist*. Their courage is not related to growth and outward development, but rather to an inward withdrawal so as to resist the harshness of the external conditions. Those who resist do not desire control, colonisation or power, but instead primarily strive to stay true to their path and, in a most special way, serve others. We should not confuse this with simple, clichéd protest: resistance is often discreet.

Resistance belongs not only to monks and hermits. In part, existence *is* resistance. Resistance expresses not a circumstantial gesture but rather a way of being, a movement of human existence. Understanding things as such, however, implies a variation in the habitual way of doing things. People have always spoken of 'resistance' but mostly in terms of resistance to things that present themselves in the face of human intentions. Ever has the earth resisted the plough — though to a lesser extent these days; dirt resisted cleanliness; the peak, its conquering. And it is from here that we get the meaning of the biblical expression: 'By the sweat of your face you shall eat bread...' The world is an arduous place, making little easy, our projects and plans often breaking against the resistance offered by reality. Indeed, 'the hard reality,' as is often said, is already a pleonasm. So then, the word *resistance* can also be used to stress not so much the difficulties the world presents before our pretensions, but the strength we might muster in the face of the processes of disintegration and corrosion that appear from both our surroundings and our very selves. For it is then that resistance manifests itself as a profound human movement.

That our existence means to resist can be demonstrated through the fact that one of the key facets of reality can be interpreted as a force of disintegration. In fact, the worst of the trials to which the human condition is subject is the constant *disintegration of being.* As if the centrifugal forces of nothingness were eager to gauge one's breaking point. Our enemies' faces may change, but the assault is eternal as it is reality itself — marked by the passing and irreversible essence of time — from which we are under siege. And from this siege do we require shelter. For those without a home, the night and the cold are the most ferocious of wild beasts to emerge from the forbidding darkness. From this we might speak of the night and the bitter cold of being, and the human warmth of the home. As faithful Kent says to a disorientated and destitute King Lear in Shakespeare's tragedy: 'Here is the place, my lord. Good my lord, enter. The tyranny of the open night's too rough for nature to endure.'[1]

To exist as to resist… It's not an immediately attractive way of looking at things, especially when compared with the dazzling and extensive inheritance left to us by existentialism through its understanding of human beings as a project. If taste were to determine the truth, it wouldn't be hard to imagine what would happen if presented with a choice between: 'to exist is to project yourself' and 'to exist is to resist.' While the notion of project engenders a sense of construction, liberty, even adventure, at first glance, the notion of resistance conjures up connotations of passiveness, immobility, even misery. Despite this, the contrast

1. Shakespeare, W, *King Lear*

between 'project' and the figure of resistance requires careful definition because, while there are contrasts, the aspects they have in common — such as the affirmation of the subject and the idea of responsibility — hold even more weight. Clearly, the idea of existence as resistance is opposed not by Sartre, but rather by the *cheap imitations* used time and again by *pseudo*-psychologists *et al* as they repeat the banal mantra: 'to live is to find self-fulfilment'. Saturated with this terminology, society has found itself distanced from Sartrean interpretation and so plays with the idea of finding one's own personal path to happiness — often understood only as achievement: in other words, success. It's not worth going into this at length here, as the sophistry of these 'experts' is not even sophistry of the good kind — that from which one can always learn — but rather excessive sophistry in that its weakness comes not from its rhetoric, but its mediocrity.

To exist as to resist… the emphasis is not on moving outward but rather on withdrawal and, for example, on the judgement that is possible only from under shelter. The silence of one who withdraws is a *methodological* silence — literally, 'of a path' — that looks for ways to see better. To refine one's senses and open them up; to be watchful; to use one's ears as eyes and eyes as ears. Could one really consider this a sterile attitude, inferior to the illusions of self-fulfilment?

If resistance is primarily present in the face of disintegration, then an analysis of the specific nature of some of our condition's most decisive entropic forces (one of which is the ever more relevant *nihilism*) is most necessary. Likewise, the analysis of the ways and causes that allow us to resist: to persevere from our adopted position or, as commonly expressed: 'to get on with things.' It is here, for example, where our experience of *home* appears in all its intensity, this time not only as shelter from the cold outdoors, but as a refuge from ice-cold metaphysical chill. Quite apart from being relative, the separation of *inside* and *outside* determined by walls and a roof does not imply closing yourself off or isolating yourself from the outside. Rather, it offers up the possibility of a way out: how might one climb the highest mountain peaks without spending a night or two in a tent or refuge? By this, we can demonstrate that resistance as withdrawal is not opposed to the idea of projecting yourself. Indeed, from this perspective, it reveals itself as its condition of possibility. By contrast, there is also an utterly sterile, aimless withdrawal and isolation, as is the case of Roquentin, the protagonist of *Nausea*: 'I for my part live alone, entirely alone. I never speak to anybody, I receive nothing, I give nothing.'[2] Neither receiving nor giving; now that really is isolation, it being the polar opposite of those who resist with an ever-willing ear out in the hope of hearing a friendly word or two, and whose generous thoughts are linked to committed action. Resistance is not *immunology*. Though Sloterdijk might disagree.

For obvious reasons, the interpretation of existence as resistance cannot be overlooked in terms of the concept's political significance. Resistance is understood colloquially as a political phenomenon consisting of the reaction of a small group of people in opposition to the domination imposed by occupation or a totalitarian government, a notorious example being that of the resistance that took place in various European countries as a consequence of Nazi occupation during the Second World War. Essentially a reaction, it is an action in the form of reaction, defence instead of offense. In the case of the European occupation, resistance meant not only defending a country or territory, but also protecting a way of life and democratic governments in the face of totalitarian ideology. Another characteristic worth mentioning from the outset is that political resistance often comes about spontaneously from the bottom up, the fruit of an awareness of what is truly at stake. To realise this does not lead one to search for 'a way out' or for individual 'salvation', but rather for a communal or social one. Because of this, those

2. Jean-Paul Sartre, *Nausea* (tr. R. Baldick), Penguin, 1963.

who resist do not do so only or primarily with themselves in mind. These, then, are the key elements for political resistance: awareness, willingness, courage and strategic intelligence so as to be able to organise and persevere despite the systematic and inevitable persecution to which those involved are subject.

Within this political register, doesn't the resisting group also perceive the illegitimate power as a disintegrating force, an imposed darkness trying to swallow up anything of any worth? Therefore, to resist in the face of tyranny and totalitarianism is to resist in the face of disintegration as, despite appearances, these regimes don't *bring together* movements of political life or knit together the social fabric, but rather homogenise all before them and impose a false, apparent whole. Those who resist are capable of renouncing creature comforts and possessions; in the extreme they are even capable of self-sacrifice. Whatever the case, what counts are the many types and distinct levels of renunciation and detachment. Those capable of giving things up in this way are able to because they know — and have experience of the fact — that 'the good life' is not the be-all and end-all: they believe in a greater good and, as such, this is no nihilism. Nor is this renunciation in the pursuit of glory or recognition from others; their position is not hoisted aloft as a banner; it is not an emblem of anything and is not used ostentatiously. Resistance leans more towards reservation than attention-seeking unless it is eventually shown to be the most suitable path towards strategic action.

The strength of those who resist comes from their more profound being. That which was already there is now expressed through resistance, and this is reflected in colloquial speech: 'They *are* a resister'. They are not simply '*acting* as a resister'; it is something that goes beyond the circumstance and uncovers a person's true being. Of course, there are certain contexts that are more likely to bring out this depth of character, thus leading those who resist to reveal themselves as such. Therefore, if it is at times true that resistance is a choice, at others those who resist simply 'find themselves resisting' without having made the decision. It is found deep within them where it has always been.

Deleuze said: 'We lack resistance to the present'. And he was right. We propose, however, to speak of resistance to the *actuality*, to the current state of affairs either imposed on us or self-imposed, and into which everything is concentrated: the disintegration of the moment and the fatality of the future. Faced with this, the resister aims simply to *not give in*. As the game is played out in the here and now, putting it off is not an option. Postponement is resignation. Perhaps later, that which has been lost can never be recovered, or the opportunity to do so will have been lost and the possibility of the impossible will then be its most definitive impossibility — basically because nobody would consider or dream of it. Memory and imagination (the idea's inner workings) are the resister's weapons of choice. Dreams, too. But not hallucination. While imagination and dreams are forces for change and for life, hallucination brings about paralysis through its deterioration of the perception that considers real that which is not: from this moment onwards, that which happens in the world lacks coherency with that which one sees or does, and from here a great numbing sets in. Yet confusion comes not only from without, but also from within the individual in such a way that the paralysis comes from both a confused world, and an equally confused 'interior'. In any case, a most urgent mandate for resistance nowadays is to not be led astray by confusion.

All resistance, and all resistance to the actuality, is therefore a portent of hope for an end that is apparently known yet all but inexpressible. Either way, one resists, and one hopes that the resistance is not in vain, though any success cannot necessarily be measured by the usual parameters. The defeat might be, or might seem to be, definitive; that said, it makes sense to keep the flame alive. The resister knows that whatever happens, their action is neither absurd nor sterile; they trust that it will bear fruit, accepting the fact that when and where this fruit will appear is unknown. They know only that preparation of this fruit comes from the edges, from the fringes.

Intimate resistance? There is no resistance without modesty and generosity. As such, its absence is validated by arrogance and egotism. Narcissus was no resister, and this must be emphasised so as to introduce the idea of 'intimate resistance'. *Intimate* not so much in the sense of inwardness, but rather in the sense of closeness, proximity, of centrality, of nuclear, of *oneself*. Intimate resistance is like electrical resistance in the sense that, paradoxically, only through resistance to its charge does it produce light and warmth to those in its vicinity. It is a light that both illuminates its own path and acts as a beacon to others, guiding without dazzling. Not a light to reveal the supreme values up in the heavens or the hidden meaning of the world, it is a light on a path that, protecting us from the harsh night, brings us clarity, affords access to nearby things, and comforts and reinvigorates us.

Intimate, therefore, is understood as proximity and nuclear. My own 'inner dialogue', the friend, the plate on the table, the home, etc., are all elements of a *philosophy of proximity* the opposite of which is not distance but rather the disconnected abstraction of life. That which is distant can, in some way, also be close while, on the other hand, it is ingenuous to speak of moving closer to the impersonal flow of information or the currents of a magnetic field. The significance of the forest, the mountains or the basements of political resistance can be found in their proximity to 'anthropological' resistance. The philosophy of proximity, while not dismissing the aforementioned, brings about a certain revindication of daily life and, as such, a revision of the all-too-common comparisons drawn between daily life and inauthenticity. It is also through proximity that the link between resistance and care is most evident. From the Socratic care of the self to Heideggerian care in *Being and Time* and the ethical nurturing of more recent times, the fact that existence is ever exposed to disintegration is common knowledge. Were this not the case, why would anyone ever take care of anything? And caring is directed specifically towards that which is close by.

Through this idea of resistance we are able to develop a reflection on two different levels that intertwine continuously. On the one hand, there is the philosophy of proximity that, as has already been mentioned, draws attention to the other (the friend, colleague, child); the air that we breathe; the food we eat; one's home; one's bedroom; the patch of sky we see from our window; our work; our daily life, etc., but also to one's own connections (our memories, feelings, hopes, etc.). Layers of intimacy, complex and variable connections acting as intimate shelter, intimate resistance; a resistance that requires neither locks on doors nor firearms for skirmishes. And on the other hand, reflective thought via this conducting thread of resistance becomes hermeneutics of the *meaning* of life; an attempt to understand the very basis of human existence. From this derive reflections on nihilism, the absurd and meaning itself.

The connection of the two discourses, both of them at times posing difficulties, allows us to continue our passage from a more theoretical level to a less abstract, more existential one. Nihilism, for example, takes on the form of exposure to the outdoors, driving those affected by it to seek out some kind of protection. Inward withdrawal, sheltering, and the identification of all that is close by function as a way of protecting us from the most elemental factors of dissolution and erosion (the exposure of existence, the passage of time, illness, ageing, etc.) in addition to the historically more variable social factors — processes of domination, violence, massification, banalization, etc... As such, social resistance is connected to 'ontological' resistance.

The fronts of resistance also oscillate between the two levels, at times without continuity. Those who resist do so by rejecting the satisfaction of the masses. Those who resist do so by rejecting the predominance and victory of selfishness and indifference, the empire of the now, the blindness of destiny, wordless rhetoric, absurdity, evil and injustice.

Those who go to the desert are not deserters. The hermit in the wasteland is in no way sterile. Life from the margins can be perfectly fruitful because what counts is the possibility of being a beginning; of each and every person being a beginning. Only thanks to not taking even a single backwards step can one hold onto the hope of meaning and open up the still clearing of peace, in the midst of immense confusion and multiple onslaughts.

II. THE CARTOGRAPHY OF NOTHINGNESS AND THE NIHILISTIC EXPERIENCE

Impelled by their adventurous spirits, the cartographers of old would set off on long exploratory journeys into unknown lands. What would they discover on these journeys? What rivers, forests and mountains would be waiting for them? After long days of travel, a virgin landscape would suddenly open up before them from the top of a ridge, their eyes contemplating it as if it were the first day of Creation. At that moment of intense joy, the hardships of the route and nights spent under precarious cover would all seem worthwhile. As would, of course, the slow but steady charting of a map that, like Chinese ink, would spread gradually across the paper.

While the cartography of nothingness is doubtless less appreciated, it is in our interests to chart it: though perhaps little more than a sketch, it should allow us to understand ourselves better, especially now that there is so little left to explore here on our planet and, paradoxically, the domain surrounding us is a source of such angst.

In the cosmological, epic literature of ancient Greece, strict nothingness played a very discrete role, the horizon of life and thought being the expiry and finality of all things. Nevertheless, it's in Greece where, with the appearance of philosophy, the question of being and, as such, of non-being, takes centre stage with writers such as Parmenides, Plato and Aristotle. In the Judeo-Christian tradition that, in a way, is little inclined towards abstraction, there are few examples of nothingness. Though those there are, are decisive. It is said that God created the world from nothing, from nothingness: 'I beg you, my child, to look at the heaven and the earth and see everything that is in them, and recognize that God did not make them out of things that existed...'[1] Though it appears later in many Latin manuscripts such as *ex nihilo*, it is here that this notion first appears. Yet Biblical discourse, more than a discourse of metaphysical speculation, is a discourse of eschatological hope. Only the combination of Judeo-Christian tradition and Hellenism would bring about the philosophical development of this question, it culminating after many centuries in Leibniz's great metaphysical question: 'Why is there something rather than nothing?' and Heidegger's contemporary reformulation of it.

But let's take a step back, as what is of primary interest to us is a map that, disappointingly for iconoclasts, requires both images and symbols. For if not these, then what?

A *well*, or *abyss*, marked in red. One doesn't fall, but might. Picture an unending freefall into the bottomless emptiness. There is nothing, nothing. Only darkness. Like when someone asks: 'Is there anything in the drawer?' And the answer comes: 'No, nothing; it's empty'. Emptiness and nothingness become synonymous, and *vacuity* is the abstract noun. As suggested by its etymology, 'no-thing' is the negation of 'every-thing,' of all occurrences, of all things: nothing for the hands to grasp, no word to be heard, no gaze to contemplate, no aroma to smell, no ground to stand on. Nothing, a void, a total absence of everything.

The hole on the map wanders, becoming increasingly unsettling. Is it moving towards us just as we move towards it? Are we so very insignificant as to be on the threshold of definitively falling into nothingness? Or are we already a part of it, with everything but a vain illusion?

In Spanish, *nada* (nothing) comes from the Latin *nulla res nata*, meaning: 'no born thing'. The fact that the evolution of the words has led to, in this case, just the word *nata* representing the

1. Maccabees 7:28, New Revised Standard Version

entirety of the original idea leads us to ask ourselves whether the truth is that everything born carries within it a nothingness that then consumes it over time, from the first day to the last. Interestingly, the Spanish *nada* doesn't require the Catalan negation of *no res*, or the English *nothing*, or the Italian *niente*, etc. As if everything that has been born is already nothing, as if the wood from which the carcass of the world is made were from the very beginning prey to the woodworm of nothingness.

Yet not only do the *well* and *abyss* wander, they progressively grow and expand. The surrounding lands gradually fall to nothingness, meaning that even as our map is created, parts of it are always disappearing. Will we have time to finish it? And if some part has already been sketched out, must it now be erased? As far as existence is concerned, the process of falling into nothingness — of 'nihilation' — affects us greatly. When Nietzsche refers to nihilism, he is primarily referring to the action, the verb, the process. Yet if a nihilistic movement or, as Nietzsche also says, a nihilistic 'logic', does exist, it must be considered in terms of how far this movement reaches and, more importantly, if there exists any kind of resistance to this logic's advance or, if once it is predominant in its domain there might remain some foothold of resistance from where an alternative movement or force might spread its roots. Either way, ever encroaching nihilism is what makes resistance plausible.

And so, we must now draw a small hut on the map: a hut to protect us from the nihilistic downpour and bolts of scorching lightning. Acting as a shelter, we wait there for the storm to pass before we rise up once again and set to tending our patch.

The remains of a *thread* to the north-east. It is tiny, the only thing we have found, and we draw it on the map as if it were the end of a half-frayed piece of string. String? The word *nihilism* is made up of the Latin base *nihil*, meaning 'nothing.' Here, etymology throws up our first dilemma: neither *nada*, nor *no res*, nor *nothing*, nor even *rien*, comes from *nihil*. The other quandary, also noted by Heidegger, is the origin of *nihil* and why it is used to mean 'nothing.' The only explanation we might have — which is still quite something, depending on how you look at it — is the following: *nihil* is composed of two words: *ne* and *hilum*, literally, 'without thread' — without relation, without conjunction. From the Archaic Latin *ne-hilum* ('without thread'), comes *nihil* meaning 'nothing.' In botany, the *hilum* is that which links the grain to the ear and the pea to the pod, it being the equivalent of the umbilical cord linking the embryo to the placenta. Clearly, important analogies arise from the image of the thread, and more specifically of the thread that unites: the thread of life, the thread in a labyrinth (Ariadne), the thread that binds (religion) …

Tugging gently on this thread, nihilism allows itself to be considered in terms that are distinct from, yet parallel to, the notion of nothingness. The nihilistic process would consist of dropping the thread, the link, the connection. Let's take a closer look at this idea. Should one wish, one can later venture further, but firstly let us consider the loss of relation. In order for there to be a connection, there needs to be two elements and a link between them. In other words, both a *difference* and a way to connect that which is different. Through words, for example. The opposite of connection is indifference, in two senses. Firstly, there is indifference as indistinction. No connection is possible if all is the same, homogeneous. Secondly, there is indifference as total disregard. Could it be, therefore, that resistance to nihilism is the defence of the difference? And could it also be that the nihilistic process provokes within us the progressive loss of connection?

An expanding well, a hut, the remains of a thread… and across a vast, marshy plain a thick *fog* spreads unerringly. Finding the path is no easy task. Where are we? Angst, like the damp fog, saturates us. We were headed north-east, but the sun is nowhere to be seen; the map is useless. Where are we? Unable to find our bearings, we are lost. From no direction, no meaning, to the absurd. The domain of nothingness is no stranger: it lingers close.

Nihilism, more than just a theoretical idea, is an *experience*. It is not enough to say it or teach it, or quote Nietzsche's (though he *must* be quoted), Heidegger's or Deleuze's thoughts. If nihilism's acidic potion, be it but a homeopathic dose, has not yet run through your veins, it will forever remain unknown to you. We must do more than repeat that, according to Nietzsche, one of the nihilistic episodes is the situation after the collapse of all our traditional values, one after another. You have to *experience* this in order to understand it and when you do, you can't help but shudder. There is perhaps no other place where thought and life reveal a fatal connection with more clarity. But this is not a notion of modal logic: deductions and reasoning, when they exist, are but secondary functions and the priority is not to follow the steps of deductive discourse as it leads us to a conclusion. From the very beginning, the experience of the fall and the abyss exists, bodies trembling, mouths agape, involuntarily gulping in nothingness. Afterwards, slightly more logical thoughts attach themselves to this experience until becoming mixed in with it. This reflection can even invigorate its protagonists — in effect, those who think — along with anyone looking for an impossible 'salvation', 'overcoming' or, at the very least, resistance. Here's an example: Nietzsche's contemporary Philipp Mainländer, a poet and philosopher with whom Nietzsche had a lot in common, wrote a philosophy of pessimism which contained statements as unsettling as the idea that the death of God had given life to the world. Claiming that *not* being was better than being, he defended virginity and suicide as a means of not contributing to the expansion of life. At the age of thirty-four, one day after the publication of his most important work, *Die Philosophie der Erlösung* ('*The Philosophy of Redemption*' — 1876), he tied a rope around his neck and hanged himself. The supremacy of nothingness was, if you will, the 'thesis' of his thoughts, though his experience of the abyss most certainly preceded this and was there, lurking in the background. Precisely because of this, rather than speak of a 'connection' between his final tragic act and his path of thought, it would be better to consider philosophy and suicide as expressions of the same experience.

We know that the nihilism advocated by Nietzsche follows in no way the same path, mostly because Nietzsche does not consider salvation to come from immersion in nothingness. What, then, is the Nietzschean experience? In *Ecce Homo*, he states that his own 'authentic experience' is that of *decline*. Because of this, and his having become a master of said experience, he says: 'a "transvaluation of all values" has been possible to me alone. For, apart from the fact that I am a decadent, I am also the reverse of such a creature.'[2] He has experienced, experiences, both sides of the coin. He experiences his decay in all of its intensity, not only in its very depths where the taste and texture of the dregs can be tasted, but also that which comes after and overcomes the previous moment. After the night, he experiences the dawn. It is understandable that most people would rather not even talk of decay (they act as if it didn't happen), while there are also some who have submerged themselves in it, never to escape. Few, very few — perhaps only Nietzsche — are capable of experiencing total disintegration before, as if as a reward, seeing that which emerges sparkling new from the fragments and dust. Here you have, therefore, the first condition by which one might fully experience it: 'But in order to feel this, one must be profound, one must be an abyss, a philosopher.'[3] Only by diving into the darkest depths of the nihilistic experience — using it all up, exhausting

2. Friedrich Nietzsche, *Ecce Homo*, (tr. A.M. Ludovici), 2016.
3. *Ibid.*

it — is one able to prescribe a solution. To entirely exhaust the experience.

Nietzsche's decay can be perfectly characterised as the physiological dissolution of the organism and a disintegration of the parts that make up the whole. This intrinsic bond between decay, disintegration and dissolution is very helpful when trying to understand a number of things. It is in our interest, therefore, to see the organic dimension of decay even before seeing its social significance. Decay is total disintegration, 'atomic anarchy', weakness and equally distributed disorder in the lower part of character and strength.

It is well-known that Nietzsche believed that decay comes from the very dawn of philosophy with Socrates and Plato and the postulation of the existence of a world of truth, different from our own. Broadly speaking, the following is the Nietzschean premise: that the form and meaning of the crisis affecting Western civilisation can be described by the word *nihilism*, and that 'decay' is the most explicit form of this crisis. The starting point of the diagnosis is understanding life as a 'will to power.' Western civilisation is in decay because it has culminated in the dominance of the weak over the strong and, as such, with the burial of will to power. A privileged example of this decay is that of the priesthood and their ability to defend within their homilies the idea that a lesser life is, at its heart, the best of all lives. In this sense, we can speak of nihilism as the domain of nothingness. Nietzsche suggests two nihilistic moments. The first corresponds to the annihilation of life as a consequence of superimposed ideals: Good, God, Reason, History, etc. (a devaluation of life as a consequence of 'superior' ideals); and the second as the devaluation of these superior ideals themselves. Deleuze calls the first 'negative nihilism', and the second, 'reactive nihilism'. A key expression from this second part is 'the death of God'. Everything with meaning that underlies life is devalued until being wiped out, therefore producing a void and general scepticism. There is no approaching finish line and no meaning attained at the end of history. Nihilism consists of a feeling of a lack of value, of realising that we can't interpret the meaning of our existence through the concepts of purpose, unity, and truth.[4] The diagnosis is followed by a proposal: the transvaluation of all ideals so as to reaffirm life. The superman is this exaltation of life and the will to power — a will to power that chooses life over nothingness. If metaphysics came about through suffering, then the Nietzschean solution doesn't consist of inventing another world, but rather creation (and the creation of what happens, which in itself is in no way long-lasting). 'The truth will set us free' is followed by '*Will* will set us free', 'the will to beget and become'.

A static character is unhelpful when understanding the movement of thought and life. Nihilism is primarily a process, a *verb* (rather than a noun).[5] The process of nihilism and the advance of nothingness. Nihilism as an historic process is, therefore, precisely that: a process that leads to nothingness (and which, in fact, comes from nothingness) at the same velocity that Man's thoughts have moved further away from life. The philosopher's task is now to think of a countermovement to resist and defeat the nihilist. That is to say, Nietzsche tries to return and invert that alienation of life back into thought, though he does so in a very peculiar way. Where could he have gone after having scaled the mountain? Well, we know that having scaled the highest peaks, there is nothing quite like going back home (to the refuge). But what if one has no home (or refuge)? Having been up there at the top, the cold creeping into the very core of

4. This is one of the best known texts: 'Looking at nature as if it were proof of the good-ness and governance of a god; interpreting history in honour of some divine reason, as a continual testimony of a moral world order and ultimate moral purposes; interpret-ing one's own experiences as pious people have long enough interpreted theirs, as if everything were providential, a hint, designed and ordained for the sake of the salvation of the soul — that is *all over* now, that has man's conscience *against* it...'
Friedrich Nietzsche, *The Gay Science*, (tr. W. Kaufman), Vintage Books, 1974
5. Within a fragment of his posthumous works, dated to the spring of 1888, we read: 'Nihilism is not the cause, but rather the logic behind decay.'

his bones, his face slashed at by the freezing wind like wave after wave of steel blades and afterwards... no shelter, no warm welcome; at the very most, a cheap imitation. Too much isolation, too many changes, bad health and aches and pains, and problems with his mother and sister (who, according to him, were the only serious objections to his thesis of eternal recurrence).

The philosophy of proximity is also an answer to nihilism, though it is very different to the Nietzschean one. It aims to resist nihilism by moving closer to finitude. Instead of eternal recurrence, there is 'returning home'. Nietzsche might say that this is nothing but a vulgar replica of the very worst of Christianity, but this is the pounding that requires *resisting*. Instead of the will to power, resistance; instead of the superman, proximity; instead of assertion, the 'problematicity'; instead of the future, memory.

ANGST, OR THE NAME OF ACCESS

Now that we have quoted Nietzsche, let's go back a step. That nihilism is primarily an experience infers that there has to be direct access to nothingness. For reference, let's use the already mentioned images of the void, the abyss, of darkness and the night (as a negation of all light and of any kind of distinction). Nothing, no thing, no occurrence, no connection, not a single word or face. It therefore seems as if nothingness is a result of negation and that we would gain access to it through the negation of all things. The *no* (from the 'there is *no*thing') would lead to nothingness.

Yet Heidegger was able to show that: 'Nothingness is more primordial than the no and negation.' Nothingness has its origins in a radical experience. If nothingness were the result of the negation of all things, it would be reduced to the result of an operation of reasoning; of an operation consisting of making a negation.

In effect, Heidegger asks if it is through negation (*no*) that one reaches nothingness: 'Is there only nothingness because of the 'not', or negation?'[6] The response is, according to him, quite the opposite, that nothingness is more primordial than both the *no* and the negation. In other words, negation exists because there was some sort of connection with nothingness before that. But then he considers how this connection works and what access to nothingness there is, as it can't be through the simple act of negation of understanding. There has to be some kind of disposition from the *self*, a state of mind, through which nothingness makes its presence felt. And here Heidegger speaks of angst as being of that essential state of mind.[7]

Of course, the notion of angst is not limited exclusively to Heidegger. Pascal, too, had already linked it to nothingness in a most incisive way:

'Nothing is so insufferable to man as to be completely at rest, without passions, without business, without diversion, without study. He then feels his nothingness, his forlornness, his insufficiency, his dependence, his weakness, his emptiness.'[8]

Here, nothingness and the void appear linked to what Pascal called *tedium* — which today we would call *angst*. He realises that in solitude man confronts his own nothingness and, in order to drag himself away from this mirror, searches continuously for amusement and activity. But escape, and especially permanent escape, is in no way a positive thing: 'I have discovered that all the

6. Martin Heidegger, *Was ist Metaphysik?* [What is Metaphysics?], (tr. translator's own)
7. It doesn't seem to me that *no* is originally a logical element either, but rather an existential element related to pain. Pain like that which is brought about by an excess of pain within the existential ambit, scandal, cries, suffering and negation. Pain would be the radical reference of the *no*. As such, we should try to nuance Heidegger: the 'no thing' is more primordial than the *no* as a logical element, but not as an expression of the experience of pain and suffering. Then, the *no* would act as an access to the nihilistic experience, taking on a character of the absurd (absurd when faced with pain) rather than that of nothingness.
8. Blaise Pascal, *Pensées*, (tr. W.F. Trotter), CCEL, 2010

unhappiness of men arises from one single fact, that they cannot stay quietly in their own chamber.'[9] To be in one's chamber or, what is essentially the same and also stated by Pascal: 'to stay with pleasure at home'. When one is capable of this, one has less need for entertainment, military adventures, and possessions, etc.

In fact, Pascal's text makes this ambiguity very clear: the home is both the problem and the solution or, at the very least, the shelter. Entertainment is characterised as a way of escape that, in the end, is a loss of oneself. People lose themselves in entertainment. And the home, solitude, is both shelter and resistance. We find ourselves, then, faced by our own personal void, our own misery, and not running from this experience is the best way of maintaining the wholeness of the subject and avoiding the loss of any more of it. Because of this, finding yourself is also ambiguous: on the one hand one is placed before one's own nothingness, and on the other hand, it is the best path towards rest.

For Sartre, *bad faith* consisted of fleeing from angst. This despite him saying: 'I flee in order not to know, but I can not avoid knowing that I am fleeing; and the flight from anguish is only a mode of becoming conscious of anguish.'[10] In *Nausea*, his most famous novel, dizziness and a mostly physiological disgust come together with the metaphysical void of one's own consciousness. In fact, in *Being and Nothingness*, Sartre says that nausea is not so much the metaphorical extract of our own physiological revulsions, but a foundation upon which all specific and empirical nauseas are produced.[11]

Angst comes from the experience of the thick, homogenous aspect of reality. Before the image of this kind of amorphous, doughy mass, the conscience is held spellbound and trapped. This distinction of captivity is precisely its pressure of disintegration: 'Everything therefore happens as if the in-itself and the for-itself

9. *Ibid.*
10. Jean-Paul Sartre, *Being and Nothingness*, (tr. H.E. Barnes), London: Routledge, 2003
11. *Ibid.*

were presented in a state of disintegration in relation to an ideal synthesis.' Reality and the spirit take part in the disintegration. This means that the assault of nothingness is not always a foreign invasion. It can come from close by or even within. As such, resistance also exists in relation to ourselves: I resist the onslaught of my own nothingness. Because of this, angst, as Sartre states, is angst before myself:

'… the recruit who reports for active duty at the beginning of the war can in some instances be afraid of death, but more often he is 'afraid of being afraid'; that is, he is filled with angst before himself.'[12]

INSOMNIA, TOO

The night and nothingness — 'Do we not stray, as through infinite nothingness? Does not empty space breathe upon us? Has it not become colder? Does not night come on continually, darker and darker?'[13]

There are three nights, each with a different meaning. The night of peace, of rest, and of dreams in which vital energy and strength are recuperated. A bed of renewal and resetting; a night in which the *self* is freed from the casing of unconsciousness, huddled low under its protective blanket. Another is that of reflection, of the voluntary vigil in which, freed from the clamour and bright lights of the day, the spirit is able to calmly contemplate the starry outer universe or its own infinite inner world. This is also a night of imagination, of guided dreaming, of adventure and epic tales. And the third is the night of insomnia, a night of involuntary vigil: a night linked to the darker forces of existence, preventing even the smallest amount of rest, holding us hostage, blind to distant forces: what constrains is unseen,

12. *Ibid.*
13. Friedrich Nietzsche, *The Gay Science*, (tr. W. Kaufman), Vintage Books, 1974

yet the bindings are tighter than ever and the impersonal dominates. This is what the philosopher Levinas analysed using the expression: *there is* (*il y a*).

The ambiguity of the night-time experience is almost constant. Firstly, it is a reversal of daytime: if the day represents transit and expiry, so the night represents permanence; if the day is effort and hardship, the night is rest. But what's more, as we have already seen, the night itself is ambiguous. Thus, the '*dark night*' found in Saint John of the Cross' *Spiritual Canticle* has a contradictory double meaning. In it, the night is all shadows and the desperation of abandoned souls, yet it is also a descent down a secret staircase, sensual trysts, a fountain, flowers... In Saint John of the Cross' poem *Noche oscura* (*Dark Night*), the night is a means of extraordinary and incomprehensible communication. There is a certain density to the night that allows a descent into the deepest depths of oneself. At times, this descent is wholly impersonal: down to a maternal core or, at times, immersed in stagnant water, dense and black. A return to primordial matter whether terrestrial mother earth or the marine mother sea. Maternity of the waters, maternity of the earth.[14] Here the blueprint of depersonalisation prevails. By day, individuality, separation and precision. By night, dissolution. Night leads to depersonalisation and postpones (provisionally or indefinitely) resistance. And, as such, it can be agreeable. It is the opposite of daytime values that makes the night: the threat of the shadows becomes a welcome while with the sounds of the day, the objects and the words, the nocturnal melodies, the fall becomes a descent: confrontation, union and return.

These are multiple ambiguities that, in fact, support different experiences. What is of interest here is not the '*divine twilight*', or even the romance of return, but rather the unnerving darkness: the night of the world and the pitch-black night of the spirit.

14. Gilbert Durand, *The Anthropological Structures of the Imaginary*, (tr. M. Sankey & J. Hatten) Boombana, 1999.

This is the night of insomnia. That which experiences the most basic equivalence between nothingness and being, revealing before the insomniac's eyes that it matters not whether there is nothingness or being, because both are charged scenarios: one charged full of nothingness, the other of being. And because of this, because they are simply full of the *same*, they are equally terrible. There is a way of thinking that identifies infinity with homogeneity. As such, we read this in Nietzsche: '... there is nothing more frightful than infinity.'[15] This is the underlying reason for a new concern. Not on a map of the earth, but rather one of the epoch in which we have now found ourselves: the age of technology. How are we to draw this era on the map? Is the age of technology monochrome? Is it a revelation of the same? Does it show us a reality that is also essentially homogeneous? If so, it would be easier to understand why Heidegger joined the age of technology with nihilism. The experience of insomnia shows us that nihilism is not only the nihilism of nothingness (or the void), but that it is equally the nihilism of the *same* (of a reality in which everything is completely equal). This and only this is the looming conundrum presented to us, not by technology, but by the age of technology.

THE NEXT DAY

The next day is no improvement. Night awaits in the background, biding its time. But things are not as they were. The deepest night of the soul is a palpable experience, permanently transforming anyone going through it so they are never the same again. A turning point has been drawn out along the trajectory of oneself, and things can never go back to how they once were. *Tragedy* — to use a classical expression — shadows us and, as observed by Unamuno and Camus, we must learn to live with

15. Friedrich Nietzsche, *The Gay Science*, (tr. W. Kaufman), Vintage Books, 1974

this feeling. Many of the superficial claims of happiness, then, are resounding in their ridiculousness.

Depending on how you look at it, personal life is an anomaly, an inconvenience, a continuous source of problems, misunderstandings, and conflicts. On what does this frail life support itself? Lifeblood runs through our veins, and at some nodal point we notice oppression. Later, our body starts to shrivel up under the weight of the gravity. Drugs and medicine offer respite, an access to the impersonal, and momentary detachment from the essence of existence.

For the next day, we need lightly packed luggage and a return to the most primordial. Etymologically speaking, this means the place where one starts the day, rising up like the sun. It acts as a guide and a source of *orientation*. This, in fact, complements Heidegger's thinking. In his opinion, nihilism is the history of the West, and as such complements its being: 'Heading west' becomes 'sunset' or 'death'. Now, this is not to be considered in an historic sense, but rather in the sense relative to the movement of human existence. Because of this, any experience of sunset or decline has to correspond to that of the origin. We have to go back to the original to rediscover our bearings. A journey to that which is more basic and more 'primordial': something that is purified of idols and all doctrinal paraphernalia is a signpost on the pathway through the mystery of existence. As the 'following day' situation comes from the very beginning of time, we have all the precedents we want: traditions of austere spirituality and philosophies of finitude and limits. 'Staying grounded,' for example, should not only be understood in the sense of a lower realism little-accustomed to imagination, but also in the realism of an especially orientating proximity.

Moment

So fundamental are the experiences of refuge or shelter, that poets who have not written about one or the other are undoubtedly few and far between. One literary reference that is especially touching — and not just because it comes from a philosopher — is Voltaire's, coming at the end of his well-known novel, *Candide: Optimism.* The book deals with a stubbornly optimistic man who, after having been beaten again and again by sad reality, eventually starts to change his opinion: 'Candide, amazed, terrified, confounded, astonished, all bloody and trembling from head to foot, says to himself: "If this is the best of all possible worlds, what are the others?"'[1] Yet the story concludes not only with a change of opinion, but with something even more important: an experience and the subsequent valuation of this experience. Essentially, having gone through the thousand and one calamities that befall him and seeing that this world is in no way what he once imagined when, as a young man, his teacher Pangloss would tell him that it was the best of all possible worlds, and after having been through all the miseries and wickedness everywhere, Candide and his friends settle down in a country house on the banks of the River Propontis. One day, they meet an old man enjoying the fresh air under the canopy of an orange tree. (He is, if I am not mistaken, one of the few sane characters in the novel). The visitors notice that the old man remains oblivious to things that happen to the great men of the city; that he is someone somewhat *out of the loop*, as we would say these days. The man confesses: 'But I never enquire what is doing at Constantinople; I am contented with sending thither the produce of my garden, which I cultivate with my own hands.' They also see that he is no great landowner, owning only one piece of land which is

1. Voltaire, *Candide: Optimism* (tr. N. Cameron), Penguin, 1997

just enough to live off: 'I have no more than twenty acres of ground, the whole of which I cultivate myself with the help of my children; and our labour keeps off from us three great evils — idleness, vice and want.' Home, land to work, and family. It is suggested that the mother is no longer with them and that, therefore, the man's children live with him. As a family they are hospitable and generous to their guests, offering them 'diverse sorts of sherbet of their own making; besides caymac, heightened with the peels of candied citrons, oranges, lemons, pineapples, pistachio nuts and Mocha coffee...'

Candide takes note and, on returning to his house, the old man still dominating his thoughts, declares: 'We must take care of our garden.' Martin, Candide's wise friend, then stresses that the key to making life tolerable is to work without thinking. Of course, this is an exaggeration: the idea is not only that work (or action) takes priority over speculation, but that there exists meaning found only in proximity. For centuries, many Eastern monasteries would only accept visitors if, in addition to adopting a series of spiritual practices, they would also be prepared to perform certain manual labours. Voltaire's story ends with Candide and his friends as they start to work their meagre property: one of them becomes a baker; another takes up embroidery; another takes care of the clothes; while yet another becomes a carpenter. Tending to plants, cooking, sewing, and making tables and chairs... all serve to survive, but also afford life a presence, a force different from that of verbose excesses. 'We must take care of our garden,' repeats Candide.

Proximity or, in Candide's case, the return to proximity (his home, his companions, his garden, intimacy, etc.) is a path towards both presence and meaning. I don't mean that he is able to completely defeat the fog of nihilism (neither Candide nor his friends can completely erase from their memories all that they have seen and experienced). The fog of nihilism can never be truly undone because it forms part of the human condition. Due to this, the meaning of proximity will never be that of a perfect, happy world. Someone might think this too modest, but there is this: it is no trick, and at times a little is a lot. 'What can save us?' asked Heidegger. And the answer is: not only a god, not just artistic creation, or even political oratory, but also *proximity*.

III. RETURNING HOME

CENTRE AND REFUGE

There are some children's games such as 'tag' or 'it' in which, having been in danger and reaching safety, the child shouts out: 'Home!' or 'Safe!'. It's worth paying attention to the satisfaction in their faces when stating these words. The equivalence is revealing: the home saves. But what does it save us from? Firstly, it saves us from the vastness. From the vastness that terrifies Pascal or that, in image form, serves Nietzsche to accentuate our insignificance. The recurring image of miniscule grains of sand lost in an infinite ocean, poised for imminent disappearance-dissolution, has its contrast in the home. The mighty, abyss-like vastness withdraws — at least momentarily — before the protection that home offers the mortal.

In a universe of unimaginable dimensions, the home is a little corner representing the centre of the world. As such, the lowly home represents more of a home than any palace of excessive dimensions. The centre requires more delimitation, more definition and, most importantly, more warmth. As Bachelard says, we need a small home within the larger one so as to experience withdrawal and a problem-free life: this is the role played by a child's den or Wendy house built out of cushions or under a table.[1] The home is an eternal symbol of *restful intimacy*. Settlement, rest, and pausing. Likewise, it is because of this that the Wendy house is more of a home than any skyscraper. There, shelter and intimate rest prevail. It is not so much about comfort or luxury, but rather withdrawal and welcome. The primordial home, also in dreams, is always more about the stay than the construction. It is always a room, and not the walls. Peace and rest require protection; and rest, for it to be so, needs to be *protected*. The profound desire for

1. Gaston Bachelard, *La poétique de l'espace* [*The Poetics of Space*], París, 1957

38

peace explains the strength of the home (that of memory, dream, or reality). 'Which of these things is more real,' asks Bachelard, 'the house where I sleep or the house in which, when sleeping, I faithfully recreate my dreams?'[2] His argument is that the dream-time home is even more radical than the physical one. 'The home from memory, the *native* home is built on the crypt of our dream-time home'. The desire for protected intimacy runs so deep as to even escape us. And it is within this subsoil that things related to the meaning of life are revealed.

Intimacy takes on the form of a receptacle, both in terms of withdrawal and satisfaction (with sustenance, sexual relations, rest, etc.) and is directly related to the home or grotto, but also to the ark or trunk, these last two having the added significance of the secret (*arcanum*). There are also mobile containers: the boat and vessel sail, true, but both are containers. As Durand states: 'Were the vessel to become a dwelling, the humblest of boats would be a cradle.' The car is, today, the heir apparent to the boat as it also functions as a mobile receptacle embracing intimacy, allowing for private gesture, even dreams.

There is a continuity between the container and its contents, this being why the container is so important when understanding intimacy. The container and its contents become synonymous with each other, and food represents this intimacy; it is assimilated and becomes akin to the same cavity. And of all foods, it is milk (the essence of maternal intimacy) and honey (for its concentration and sweetness) that stand out and can remind us of a now long-gone primordial intimacy.

There is also an element of secrecy. The intimate is the most clandestine of all, the intimate of the intimate; like the philosopher's stone or the elixir of life. The purest concentration. The extract. From here comes the isomorphism of gold, or even salt.

2. Gaston Bachelard, *Earth and Reveries of Repose : An Essay on Images of Interiority*, (tr. M. McAllester Jones), DIP, 2011

Both of them are the result of a *concentration* and are 'centres'. The path to intimacy is a path to mystery, secrecy, towards treasure, rest and sustenance. Here, on the other hand, the opposite direction to that of intimacy is that characterised by difficulty, hardship, deterioration, dispersion and even exhibitions of hostility. For a long time (and for too many people, even now), to live meant striving to survive, employing all of one's strength to do so. In richer societies, however, this push to survive has given way to something else: the struggle not to disintegrate. And while the apparent enemy is much less terrible, failures and defeats are all the more frequent.

The home, as a centre, stops the world from descending into chaos or dispersion; it is the condition by which the world exists. And the horizon glimpsed from a window is the clearest symbol of this representation: 'To see the world through a keyhole'. Withdrawal, and withdrawal in the comfort of the home, is necessary to both 'see' and 'observe' the world. In other words, it's just as important to have it or touch it with one's gaze as it is to follow — this being the meaning of *observe* — and be guided by it. Of course, this is because neither looking nor following are particularly sophisticated intellectual exercises, but rather guidance methods required to live. As such, the home, together with the you, is the most relevant point of reference. It is spatial: 'far from home', 'close to home'; and emotional: 'like home' or 'the memory of home.'

The home is a discrete centre of the world, centralising it. And while the home is the heart of the world, the hearth is the heart of the home. It warms, and is where saucepans boil and people meet to warm themselves and converse. While in no way naturally geometric, it is rather existential, bringing together and guiding.

At times, the importance of return can go unnoticed, precisely and paradoxically because it is always expected. Indeed, only when return is not possible do we think of and miss it. *Returning home*. As an expression it is, in fact, somewhat redundant because the home is already defined as 'a place to return to'. A home isn't a place to go to, but rather return to, and one tends to return home every day. But temporary return only, not everlasting. The philosophy of the home is not that of everlasting return, but rather return; a return that, while repeated, is finite in number. The insupportable hardship of the eternal recurrence contrasts its sweetness. Though perhaps nothing more than a foreboding, we know that one return will be our last. Life is a parable of returns.[3]

The return home, however, carries within it something of the impossible. Firstly, because home itself is a dream (it has never been this perfect) and secondly because the nihilistic experience cannot be overcome. Its shadow is never far away. The modern-day Odysseus returns having travelled through the land of the void, returning only after a devastating earthquake has cracked the modest bedrock of his spirit.

The human spirit is a yearning to return, this leading Novalis to state that philosophy is a nostalgia for being at home. Yet we have never been to the home to which we wish to return.

In the home we do have, grace doesn't lie in staying at home from the off, or in leaving never to return, but rather the act of return. Under careful consideration, the act of staying at home is impossible, carrying as it does the heavy cost of self-betrayal. Narcissism is a most sterile stillness, lacking all life. As one has not left, one cannot return. Leaving not to return is no betrayal, but it is a loss. And ecstasy without return has only two possibilities: gradual bacchanalian disappearance or illness and suicide.

3. See the film *The Road Home* (1999), by the Chinese director Zhang Yimou.

The return is motivated not only by exile or being lost, but is related to a fundamental crack, the difference being its origin within our consciousness. As such, *reflection* is one of the ways we might return.

The concept of return has been around for as long as we have walked the earth. And not just because it's the key to the synonym between the earth and home. Life is a separation from the horizontal earth, and death is a return home, leading us to this desire to be buried in mother earth. Through burial, the earth becomes our second, then immemorial, cradle. Yet return comes about according to specific circumstances of each moment. Now, the return is from the midst of a society of distraction, speed and impersonality.

What does this return tell us about the *who*? How is the *who's* way of being expressed as home? Does the home invite us to connect to the idea of the interior? Or rather to the experience of intimacy? The question is rhetorical as we have chosen intimacy as a milestone on our path from the outset, and we must continue to do so. The notion of *inside* is simply one of the ways to describe the return and, as such, the notion of intimacy is a lot richer and more versatile than the inside. *Interior* means a part on the inside, a part on the outside and a separation; *intimacy* indicates proximity, familiarity. As such, *at home*, is a much more adequate term than 'in the home'.

This 'at home' reminds us to employ the slightly vague terms *intimacy, familiarity*, and *proximity*. They indicate something in no way related to possession or property, but rather protection and refuge. 'My house' tugs in this direction, and not in the fidelity of the possessive. Neither the house, nor you, nor even the soil (in its radical sense) are possessions. As such, while people are still able to talk about things in terms of property (*my house, my children*, etc.), in reality the possessive here expresses identification and proximity: for example, 'I am of this house or I have a duty to my children'. There also remains a secondary question of use. It is obvious that a house serves a purpose, but it first and foremost acts as a guide and as familiarity. A house's instrumentality is preceded by and integrated into both the way the human being is and that of proximity and refuge. The house does not act as a refuge, but rather like the human, its way of being is that of a refuge.

GIVING

The house represents the concavity of the shelter in the same way that a handmade bowl is that of the act of giving. The roof of a house takes the form of two hands pointed downwards; the palms constitute the ceiling. The bowl is made with two hands pointed upwards. The bowl offers and gives. The roof protects and shelters. The shelter leads us to the act of giving. What is given at home leaves home to give. In effect, it is the house that accompanies (as a condition or as an intention) the act of giving rather than any kind of exchange. This is why it is so difficult to undertake a philosophy of giving. It is worth examining how Derrida links hospitality and this act. Speaking — paradoxically — of the impossibility of giving (this doesn't mean that it doesn't exist, but rather that it is not possible for it to appear as such), so does he relate it to hospitality and occurrence. Without doubt, the best access to this notion comes from people who give and, most importantly, give *themselves*. The order of the *Fraticelli* or 'Little Brethren' gave everything, at times going back to their convent — also open to all and sundry — naked, as they had given away their clothes. Even with the Fraticelli, the possibility of return forms the foundations of giving. Discussions about the act of giving (and an economy of this act far removed from the late-capitalist logic of consumption) should not — must not — settle for abstract, moderately sophisticated speculation or the reiterated and already unnecessary criticism of the perversions of consumption for consumption's sake and 'indefinite growth' lacking shape or horizon. One's hands must be used and one must witness, once again, the gesture. There is a story about a charitable friar towards the end of the 19th Century called Leopoldo d'Alpandeire who would go from door to door asking for alms for the poor. On one occasion, he knocks on a door and a man comes out and spits on the good friar's outstretched hand. 'That's for me,' replies the friar, his hand still slightly outstretched and cupped in the hope of receiving something he could then pass on, 'now give me alms for the poor at the orphanage.'

This is worth emphasising: we take the food bowl with our hands, but the concavity of our hands forms the first bowl, gathering and holding. Ever the stretched-out, recipient-shaped hand or the embrace: these are the fundamental gestures of the philosophy of giving.

To give yourself is to serve others in terms of food, company, tenderness or shelter. From here come alms and charity houses or hospitals. Altruism is house-shaped and an unwelcoming house is no house at all. Because of this, a house is never quite finished. The economy of giving does not have its eye on progress, but rather perseverance and repetition. That everyone might have a home and food. Even the word — bowl-like — gathers and receives.

The physical act of giving is close to that of gathering. They are both gestures and movements of existence that are neither expansion nor isolation. To gather is to collect so as to keep safe, and to welcome and provide refuge is to safeguard and gather yourself, to not get lost or dispersed. To marry is to unite. To gather and withdraw are gestures of the giver. There where Deleuze creates a philosophy of folds, here we write of *withdrawal*, it being not so much a variation, but rather an alternative. Folds don't tend to have a centre; withdrawal does. Folds come from plans and allow us to consider multidimensionality, while withdrawal comes from the action of withdrawing yourself. Folds are composition: withdrawal is simplicity. Folds, exteriority: withdrawal, the act of removing yourself from outside ('removal', withdrawal). Withdrawal is at the same time both the prologue and the epilogue of the act of giving.

METAPHYSICS OF THE HOME

Throughout the history of Western thought, metaphysicians, both those who have focussed on the theory of the basic principles of being and those dedicated to understanding the movement of the absolute spirit, have made few concessions to the layperson. If one were to interview one of these metaphysicians, asking them to produce a philosophical reflection starting with the following statement: 'The roof allows the storm to pass over without washing away those sheltering below', it's quite possible that they would exclaim: 'And what does any of that have to do with metaphysics?' Metaphysics has sought out permanence without taking into account the concept of shelter (in terms of human circumstance, shelter would be viewed as 'merely relative'). The substance, the implicated being, the metaphysics of possible worlds, the eternal recurrence, etc. All have a single common denominator: *permanence without shelter*. Is there, however, any other possibility for metaphysics? What would happen if we were to pay attention to the fact that human permanence is sheltered permanence? Metaphysics would then find itself confronted by the notion of home, the refuge of existence. And so, let's unravel this thread. Both the Hebrew word *bavith* and the Arabic *buit* mean 'haven' and 'house'.[4]

With the house, the metaphysics of substance could give way

4. Using this etymological root, José Ángel Valente wrote a beautiful piece called *Bet*, where we can read: 'House, place, bedroom, dwelling; this is how the shadowy narrative of time starts: for something to have endurance, imagination, presence: house, place, room, memory: the hand makes the concave and centres the extension...'
José Ángel Valente, *Noventa y nueve poemas*, (tr. translator's own), Alianza, 1981

to that of shelter, and would therefore stay in the background of the Nietzschean criticism of metaphysical history as a Platonism; a criticism, at its core, of the idea of substance. But we are well aware that this has not stayed in the background. With the metaphysics of substance now dead and buried, there seems to be nothing left standing, nothing durable and, therefore, nothing meaningful. The supposed permanence of the metaphysical world has been substituted for the variability and change of the unique world. Contrary to this, with the idea of home we would progress differently. All homes are precarious and of this world: nothing of the Platonism criticised by Nietzsche, then. And yet permanence takes on its meaning through the experience of the home. Post nihilistic metaphysics, returning to its origins, has to start being a metaphysics of the home. Permanence not thanks to substance and identity, but rather to shelter and care. Where would it take us?

The mortal wants to resist, even only provisionally. Everything, from the most exuberant to the most discreet, from the strongest to the most fragile, everything is destined to disappear; to be dissolved away by the implacable passage of time, swallowed up in the darkness of the world. Everything, human beings included, has the tragic gift of seeing it coming. We are, as we say, aware of our finite nature. To die, to pass away. This awareness of our finite nature — no obsession, but rather the sincerest of all reflections — does not lead one to overcoming it. It leads one to resist. Derrida calls it *demeure*, indicating not only the place where one remains, but also the action of remaining, of staying there.[5] To *delay* is just as much being late as it is to spend time in a place. It is linked to both meanings: staying put in some place and delaying the conclusion. The Latin for *delay* is *demorari*, meaning *to wait* and *to take time*. 'There is always a notion of waiting, of contretemps, of delay, of dilation, of extension [both] in terms of *demeure* and moratorium...' To live is to survive; *to survive* is in no way derived from *to live*; rather, the opposite is

5. Jacques Derrida, *Demeure*, (tr. E. Rottenberg), SUP, 2000

true. In an interview published under the title 'On the Word', Derrida says: 'I don't know if to survive is a categorical imperative, I think it's the same form as both experience and unrenounceable desire'. *To survive* is to delay the moment of death but, at the same time, it goes further than death. The meaning of home doesn't succumb with the arrival of death.

THE WELCOME

The metaphysics of the home should come accompanied by an *ontology of gestures*, of methods, of gestures. Within communities of shelter, hospitality and love, ways, acts and gestures are considerably more essential than objectifications such as contents or structures. A house of words and gestures. The essential gesture is that expressed by the verb *to shelter*, meaning: 'to protect; conceal; defend'. And being unsheltered means finding yourself without protection, help or assistance and the home is the most emblematic expression of what it means to shelter and protect.

When speaking specifically about the movements of human existence, Jan Patočka, the great contemporary Czech philosopher, refers to the movement of welcoming to highlight the fact that the most essential act of welcoming comes from one's fellow being. The other is the primordial home:

'As such, from the beginning of his life, man finds himself immersed, rooted, in the other. Rooting yourself in another affects the other relationships. From the very beginning, it is the other who takes care of our *needs* [...]. They are the *other* and, in terms of natural, necessary, reciprocated bonds, it is thanks to the *others* offering me cover and help that, for me, the land can be land and the sky, sky: the others are the primordial *home*.'[6]

6. Jan Patočka, *The Natural World as a Philosophical Problem*, (tr. E. Abrams), NUP, 2016

Human existence starts in the *house that is the other*. As such, the other is the fundamental reference point and that which makes the other two (the heavens and the earth, or temporal and spatial orientation) possible. The you, the earth, the sky; with the you taking priority. 'Your' region or neighbourhood: one might believe that *region* or *neighbourhood* alludes primarily to land, a geographic delimitation. If this were the most important determination, then the fact that poetic discourse evokes the act of laying down roots in a place, telluric attractions, aesthetic fascination with landscape and even patriotic abstraction might be predictable. But no. *Neighbourhood* is a noun deriving from *neighbour*, itself coming from the Old English *neahgebur*, which is a compound of *neah* 'near' and *gebur* 'dweller'. That which makes a neighbourhood and therefore a wider region is not so much the land, but the you, the other. Each person's territory is that which is given by others according to the proximity in which they appear in the midst of the earth and the heavens. Human territory, therefore, is simply a meeting point.

'The introduction of novelty in the world', as Hannah Arendt defines the specifically human occurrence of childbirth, cannot be considered as being on the margins of a primordial welcome as the welcome itself is a condition of existence. That said, one might reflect on the different tones this welcome represents, while never ignoring the fact that it is in no way simply relative or merely circumstantial. One must view the tenderness and care of the welcome. Of this, it has been said — despite the misunderstandings this might provoke — that the welcome has a 'feminine' character. Obviously, this character has nothing to do with female seclusion within the home (*oikos*), and exclusion from the excellence of the public space (*polis*). It does, however, have a lot to do with maternity, though especially in terms of the difference between that which drives the embrace and that which comes from the blow (of an axe, for example). While 'masculinity' has a worldly, expansive function, the mother's arms represent the first cradle.

Our movement of intimacy, therefore, cannot be colonial, imperial or totalitarian. Though perhaps the 'outer' home is rectangular, on the inside the angles tend to become curves, with the curving of the angle representing femininity. The rectangle signifies a relation with resistance in the face of external aggressions and the instruments of aggression, whereas curved roundness is related to fruit, the maternal womb, tenderness, peace and security.

EXTERIORITY AND POLITICS

The main match is not played between the *intimacy-exteriority* coupling. It is not the case that resistance is an exercise of fortifying the intimacy, nor is it that taking care of oneself is a strictly centripetal movement. In the very best of cases, existence is always exposed, open and interpolated. The path of bidirectional intimacy-exteriority is the path of existence. To bar the way supposes a reduction, an impoverishment, a loss. Therefore, the question does not lie between the interior or the external, but rather what kind of transit there is between them, what kind of relationship they have. One thing is consumerist fascination, in which the eroticism of goods sucks on an intimacy that is predisposed to dispersion, while another is the communication with others and the construction of the world. Intimate resistance, therefore, does not allude to closure. They are not walls, but openings, gaps, that link one to the exteriority. You return home only because you have left.

As such, the philosophy of the return home does not turn its back on politics: it is not a neglect of politics. In fact, superficial politics is often due to little or no intimate resistance, it taking advantage of the weakness of the home. The proliferation of self-help guides runs parallel to the proliferation of ever more banal politics. And both progressions are due to the disintegration of oneself.

What's more, the gesture the hands make when gathering

resembles not only the embrace but also the gesture that defines and maintains the community, and this community requires an urgent rethinking. But how might we do this, beyond neoliberal one-dimensionality, communist abstraction and communitarian restrictions? The home and giving (or generosity) are good places to start, as well as the movements of gathering and bringing together (represented by the town or village hall), producing axes of connection.

THE HOUSE OF THE SPIRIT

We will attempt to explain the idea of the home as it corresponds to human *conjunction* in the next chapter. It has foundations and windows: the foundations and basement link it to the earth; and the windows and attic to the air, daytime, and the heavens. The home unites the earth and the heavens, but human conjunction is, first and foremost, shelter. Home is a comforting word, warming both body and spirit. Because of this, the deepest nostalgia and hope is that which is submerged in the universe of infancy and the home. Regarding this subject, I feel that you would be hard pushed to find anything more inspirational than these lines from Czech writer Vladimir Holan's poem 'Resurrection':

> Is it true that after this life of ours we shall one day be
> awakened by a terrifying clamour of trumpets?
> Forgive me God, but I console myself
> that the beginning and resurrection of all of us dead
> will simply be announced by the crowing of the cock.
>
> After that we'll remain lying down a while...
> The first to get up
> will be Mother...We'll hear her
> quietly laying the fire,

quietly putting the kettle on the stove
and cosily taking the teapot out of the cupboard.
We'll be home once more.[7]

7. Vladimír Holan, 'Resurrection', (tr. unknown)

IV. A EULOGY TO THE DAY-TO-DAY: THE SIMPLE LIFE

Let us imagine that one day, fortune would appear and offer one of us the immeasurable gift of meeting an angelic creature. Its friendly demeanour would no doubt lead to a relaxed, un-rushed conversation. Truly good dialogues cannot be predicted, as everything depends on the first few words and the capacity to listen. Of course, in a situation as improbable as this, a fundamental worry would probably raise its head at one moment or another: perhaps with the conversation already underway, the mortal might express their anxiety regarding the meaning of life and the problem of pain and suffering. A literary example of this can be found in the Pere Quart's theatrical work *Allò que tal vegada s'esdevingué* (*That Which Once Happened*), in which the protagonist Caïm asks the angel Querub a number of shrewd questions. Of course, as we have demonstrated, were the conversation between the angel and us prolonged and relaxed, then both speakers would probably — if there is anything probable about this conversation — be interested in the life of the other. Perhaps the angel, faced by the mortal's curiosity, would tell them something about celestial objects and events never before seen on earth. But when, in deserved reciprocity, it was the human's turn to tell the angel something, what extraordinary thing could the mortal say so as to awaken the angel's interest? Perhaps, at first, they would talk about magnificent events and monumental works but, after a while, seeing that these weren't cutting the mustard, the mortal would realise that, for the angel, the most interesting thing would be something that, for us, would be the most obvious or ordinary. In the eyes of an angel, the simple routine of our daily lives would be more 'extraordinary' than anything else. It is precisely what Rilke beautifully recommends in the ninth part of his *Duino Elegies*:

'Praise the world to the Angel, not the unsayable: you can't impress him with glories of feeling: in the universe, where he feels more deeply, you are a novice. So, show him a simple thing, fashioned in age after age, that lives close to hand and in sight. Tell him things. He'll be more amazed: as you were, beside the rope-maker in Rome, or the potter beside the Nile.'[1]

Just that: 'show him a simple thing'. At times, we should also be the angel listening and watching, as if for the very first time, the simplicity of our daily lives as pointed out and told by ourselves. Let us avoid ever seeking out the extraordinary, rather admiring ourselves from the point of view of the simple, learning to value it as it is. Depending on how you view it, it's the most sublime of it all. Here is a good lesson that is well within our reach and, perhaps because of this, one of the most difficult to learn. For those of us unable to dispense with our books, Chekov and Kierkegaard (who writes about the sublime in the pedestrian) are masters of this lesson. To make daily life and the simplicity of it our own (though not in the sense of taking possession) in some way 'saves us'. And with that, all would be said and done, though it's worth going through it step by step.

If we take its meaning literally, daily life is the life that we experience most days and, because of this, the most common characteristics of everyday life are repetition and routine; though not exactly the repetition of that which is identical — which would be both sinister and insufferable — but rather *similar* repetition in the sense of a mix of what is already known and that which is vaguely new. A couple might have a child. The day of the birth will, without doubt, be an incredibly special, extraordinary day — one does not have a child every day. But as of this moment, the child will be present in the lives of the couple, forming part of their everyday lives. Because of this, one occasionally hears about the 'burden' of having a child, not only in terms of the attention they require, but because even if we wanted — which is never the case — we are unable to offload

1. Rainer Maria Rilke, *Duino Elegies*, (tr. A.S. Kline), 2004

them. They will be with us forever. Though, of course, not always in the same way. Daily life is a kind of synthesis in which a certain variation appears and integrates itself. As such, in order to characterise it, referring to it as 'mere routine' or 'mere repetition' does not really fit the bill. There is a contrast between the 'every day' and the 'one day after another', the previously mentioned synthesis of experience and the new sitting alongside each other in discrete hope. The contrasts are clear: working days, days of rest; effort and weariness, respite and leisure; daydreaming and staying grounded, etc. Only the day of rest turns daily life into daily life. And then the day of rest itself forms part of normality and the cycle. One day of rest links up with the next, sandwiching daily life between them. It is not a time out, but rather the moment of rest that confirms the effort of the day to day. As if daily life were the school, and the holiday a pause suitable for reflection, for thought, for giving thanks, for rest, for withdrawal and for enjoyment. On the other hand, workdays are, strictly speaking, time, and time is effort: one awakens and is faced by one's daily tasks. The same contrast exists between night and day. The night and rest are invitations to let yourself go, and we abandon ourselves to sleep. Sleep is both rest and freedom from the weight and effort of the day. While the act of suicide has more than once been associated with the model of sleep, there is an enormous difference: sleep's liberation is first and foremost recovery for the next day. Beyond the relationship with the effort-rest binomial, contrast plays a leading role. If it's you who takes on the day (doing what the day demands of you), at night you are not the one piloting the ship. Rather, it is you who is piloted. You continue breathing, but it is as if life were breathing you or for you. Night surrounds and absorbs you. Later, morning arrives and you wake up. Just as the day starts, so does the self: and the self has things to do. There's no time at night. It starts with the day, at the 'same time' as the effort and movement established by the self.

While the day's constituents are related to working effort, they are also connected to the satisfaction of necessities and the maintenance of human relations. In all of this, there is the contrast between difficulty and satisfaction. There is pleasure in the satisfaction of the most basic necessities: for example, in eating, resting, sexual relationships; but also in conversations, coexistence, in daydreams and distractions, etc. And difficulty is not only relative to work, but also to conflicts of recognition and competition with others, to disappointment, inverse expectations, etc. There is a difficulty linked to the instant: as if every moment required a small effort that, over time, produced the undeniable fatigue of the day. The movement of existence does not unfold without effort; it is as if time itself were dense, as if the path were always slightly inclined upwards. Moving is difficult, as is breathing, as is pouring water into a glass, as is tolerating the lies within the context… But more than anything, it's day to day illness, oppression, and misery. Escape and evasion in the form of distraction or dreams explain, in part, these difficulties.

So as to typify daily life, to the characteristics of repetition, joy, and difficulty must be added the most decisive element of them all: proximity. To do so, however, we must first of all ask ourselves where the idea of daily life as a second-class, inferior life has come from. Without doubt, one of the factors is that of the doomed romantic, with their celebration of exceptional lives, both in form and intensity. The romantic hero might die young but, if nothing else, they have stood out and escaped from the anonymous average of the common mortal. Today, for better or worse, this model of romanticism is less present, though it has not been exchanged for a more adequate attention to daily life. In this society of appearances, all we have been left with is the vainglory of underwhelming hierarchic power or the verbal diarrhoea associated with mass media, and day-to-day life remains pushed aside. Traditional social models were elitist, as are the romantic and media models (as an even larger number of people are required to applaud celebrities.)

With some exceptions, contemporary philosophical discourse has mostly failed to underline the value of day-to-day life, more often than not devaluing it. Heidegger contributed decisively to its discredit. And here we must pause because, as ever, dialogue with Heidegger enriches our approach as his *Being and Time* leads us to the identification between daily life, indifference and the fall into inauthenticity and impropriety. The meticulous reader, however, might have to dig a little deeper as Heidegger also states that: this indifference towards *Dasein*'s everydayness is a positive phenomenal characteristic of this *entity* (ens), it being the starting and ending point of all of the most authentic forms.[2] For Heidegger, everydayness is not an accidental phenomenon that one might leave behind forever, but rather a fundamental, constitutional phenomenon from which a more appropriate, more suitable movement would emerge: the movement of existence. It is clear, however, that within this blueprint, daily life represents the greatest shortfall; as such, Heidegger attributes to it this indifference, mediocrity and anonymity. In daily life nobody is — strictly speaking — oneself. That's to say, someone who speaks or acts from and for oneself, but rather that what one says and does has a lot to do with what is usually done or usually said. Thus, Heidegger states that, in daily life, the oneself of *Dasein is a self*, not *one's own self*. In other words, a oneself that has been purposefully assumed. Therefore, I have to assume something of myself for it to properly be. Daily life is *remaining* in daily life, precisely so as not to have to confront it. The overriding convenience of leaving daily life is manifested in this passage where, among other things, Heidegger speaks about a double possibility of succumbing: 'In everydayness *Dasein* can undergo dull 'suffering', sink away in the dullness of it and evade it by seeking new ways in which its dispersion in its

2. Martin Heidegger, *Being and Time*, (tr. J. Macquarrie & E. Robinson), Harper & Row, 1962

affairs may be further dispersed.'[3] If appropriation is an escape from everydayness, then there is another, much easier path to take: that of evasion.

There are two paths so as to not 'overcome' everydayness: submerge yourself in it or evade it. This second one, evasion, is a way of increasing dispersion, heaping dispersion onto dispersion. But what are we trying to evade? There is something apparent in daily life that we can either confront so as to make it ours or run from. As already mentioned, Heidegger believes our most fundamental way of being is our own being-towards-death, and that to accept this means a deepening of the awareness of our own mortality. We are not a thing, not even anything we might conceive of as falling into a category of substance. In fact, the world of things knows not death, only transformation. Awareness of death is awareness of the end, the nothingness of existence. Awareness calls us to the being-towards-death, which is the same as saying that it calls us to existence, or the same as saying that it calls us to truly be. This awareness contrasts with the 'fall' that consists of considering yourself as being a thing among things. *Fallen* means 'being among things, wrapped up warm and protected by them all' (by the things, by the customs, by everything that fulfils and determines everyday life). But angst drags one away from his fall and drives him towards inhospitableness, and away from the home (*Unheimlichkeit*). It's as if the revelation of *Dasein*'s Being-towards-death was already provided by its own way of daily being. And it's because of this that it can escape, increasing dispersion, evading itself: 'Having been thrown into Being-towards-death, *Dasein* flees — proximally and for the most part — in the face of this thrownness, which has been more or less explicitly revealed.'[4] Thrownness (*Geworfenheit*) is essentially related to death, and is not thrownness into the world (this would be more along the lines of Ortega). The fall,

3. *Ibid.*
4. *Ibid.*

like dwelling between things, is an escape from thrownness. Not in the sense of escaping from the inhospitableness of the world, but rather the inhospitableness of ourselves. There are different ways of escaping. One of these is curiosity. Curiosity is related to wanting to see; not with the desire to see so as to understand more, but rather the desire to see so as to lose it quickly from sight and continue longing for the new. Curiosity and novelty lead to an inability to calm yourself, to continuous forward flight.

With this, we clearly have to agree with Heidegger. Evasion is not evasion of the world, but rather of my own self, from the nothing that I am, from the mortal being I am. This nothingness has also been called the *abyss*. The difference with Heidegger primarily consists of the characterisation of *daily life not as falling, but as an inherent answer to the abyss*. This means that through the use of the term, *daily life* doesn't allude to the same thing and that the divergence is mostly terminological.

To assume the mantle of our own existence doesn't mean, in fact, distancing ourselves from our daily lives. Where would we go? Nor does it mean leaving behind the world of things. Rather it consists of relating ourselves to it without dispersion, having assumed the whole of existence, recognising ourselves as finite beings and letting things come to light that project this finitude. Heidegger, in his *Letter on Humanism* calls this a *clearing*, an open space where things can make themselves present. The ecstasy of existence consists of this clearing, affording us proximity to things; a proximity that is not only that of utilisation, or that provides contemplation, but rather that of the company that brings together. The table, window and belfry accompany us, but we don't feel like just one thing amongst many others, but like the existence uniting them.

That we will not be talking of *clearing*, but of *conjunction* has already been anticipated, but I share Heidegger's attention to proximity, which is something I employ so as to define daily life. A proximity, as we have already shown, that is revealing, but at the same time guiding. A proximity to objects, to the earth, to the heavens and, most importantly, to the you. The centrality of the other in both the western and eastern horizon. 'To lose one's way' is to lose that fundamental orientation: the day and its adjacent silhouettes, gestures, everyday words and, most importantly, the face of the other that accompanies us. Disorientation is the momentary loss of all of this. It is not just a spatial: 'Where am I?' In regard to that which is most important, primordial proximity is indispensable. The crux — or backdrop — of existence isn't hidden beyond proximity, but rather within it, in the middle of it, within its protection. Proximity is not an escape from one's own inhospitableness; proximity is a place that avoids neither inhospitableness (the abyss) nor the angst that it reveals. But the echoes of this are softened by the velvety character of proximity and the warming skin of one's fellow being.

Our existing is to remain in proximity, caring instead of controlling. To accompany and care for are expressions of proximity, everyday life's most distinctive trait. Is this so different from what Heidegger says? Not at all. His is also a sustained, untiring effort towards proximity. A scene to which he alludes says it all. It is a quote from a text by Aristotle that, in turn, refers to Heraclitus:

'The story is told of something Heraclitus said to some strangers who wanted to come visit him. Having arrived, they saw him warming himself at a stove. Surprised, they stood there in consternation — above all because he encouraged them, the astounded ones, and called to them to come in, with the words, "For here too the gods are present".'[5]

The strangers assumed that they would find Heraclitus (notably wise as he was) in a most unique situation due to his renowned excellence and, what do you know, instead they find him in one of the most typical winter situations possible: warming himself

5. Martin Heidegger, *Letter on "Humanism"*, (tr. F.A. Capizzi), Routledge, 1978

by the fire. In that moment it's as if the strangers were disappointed: they were expecting something exceptional and what they are faced with is an everyday occurrence. They were going to visit Heraclitus in the same way tourists these days go to visit an exotic country, avidly searching for novelty, for marvellous things (worthy of explaining afterwards), and they are confronted instead with a completely normal scene. They don't realise that Heraclitus' wisdom has nothing to do with situations or strange atmospheres. They are not able to grasp what Heraclitus is showing them: that within this everyday proximity there lies that which is most admirable; that there, too, resides the divine. The difference between Heraclitus and the strangers is that while Heraclitus is capable of grasping the depth of daily life because he has expressly accepted its own finite nature, the strangers have not. They search near and far — inside and out — for that of which, at that moment, they are incapable. And it's not that wise people like Heraclitus don't travel. They could. But while understanding and experiencing the journey in a different way. What would they make of the current restlessness of the modern-day? Once again, there is an obsession with travelling that clearly responds to a yearning for novelty. How often do people travel great distances only to see nothing, or to continue their constant chatter, or to forget our finite condition, or because they're bored and don't know what to do, or to escape from themselves, or to search for an illusory freedom, etc.? The discomforting content of immanence without proximity demands this restlessness, and here you see that the more restless we are, the further we are from the world.

Let us emphasise this: the appropriation of daily life is that which we understand here as daily life. But *appropriation* is an effort. Heraclitus next to his stove represents the appropriation of daily life and its revindication. The appropriation of daily life also means the revelation of the primordial, the revelation that comes from breaking bread. For those who return home and sit at table, we are presented with the most sublime of all things. That which has no name, the primordial of the primordial, reveals itself in the moment of repetition with the fellow diner. In *The Human Condition*, Hannah Arendt speaks of the repetition of labour as that which we do so as to satisfy the cyclical necessities of life. Through this, she analyses the futility of products of consumption. In being eaten, the apple is consumed, and the same thing happens, by definition, with all of the other foodstuffs and things destined to satisfy our necessities. There would be nothing left to say of this analysis were it not for the fact that it gets nowhere near the depth of daily life. Consumable goods, as they are, have very little to do with proximity. On the other hand, when Arendt refers to objects, to usable goods, to the table and the home, only then does she refer to the possibility they offer our process of identification (that which surrounds us helps us to identify ourselves). Yet with all of this, no attention is paid to the most essential: the primordiality that is linked to proximity. It cannot explain that that which is seen on a daily basis from the same window or the aroma one smells when sitting down at table are occurrences born of the primordial, there where the human being is at their truest. It doesn't pick up on the mystery that the everyday hides. Arendt says: it's the table, that which lasts (some things made by mortals last longer than their own short lives, and because of this, humans identify themselves with their works). It's true, but the gesture, the act of sharing lasts longer still. Nothing lasts longer than daily repetition. Arendt believes that the world of things partly sustains the transience and change in mortal lives. True. But it sustains it because this ever more centralised world is made up of the daily gesture. It's not the table, but rather our arms leaning on it time after time, our hands breaking bread and passing the salt to and fro. To share a table is to share a meal, but the meal goes a lot further than the physiological dimension of eating. At table, fellow diners also feed themselves on gestures and words. The meal enjoys a particularly rich symbolic significance. It is no coincidence that the Eucharist, a ritual meal in remembrance of Christ's actions, is the supreme symbol of the Christian religion. Nor is it a coincidence that in many utopias the imaginary society frees itself from conflict, misery and death through the representation of the meal.

We can agree with Heidegger when, in commenting on Hölderlin, he says that everything that sustains itself requires roots. But what kind of roots? Heideggerian terrestrial rooting is just one possibility that was unfortunately sullied by his references to blood and land in his shameful letters and lectures from darker times. There might, on the other hand, be a different kind of rooting: a rooting in the day and its gesture, rooting in day-to-day company, rooting not in impersonal elements, but rather in human warmth.

To the angel, then: 'show him a simple thing, fashioned in age after age, that lives close to hand and in sight'. It wouldn't be too difficult, as the angel would easily recognise the miracle of daily life, perhaps even envying the proximity and simplicity that it brings.

Proximity to things and others doesn't sit well with abstractions. It's strange that today more than ever we lack tangibility. Because of this, the need for a new kind of materialism is notorious: one which hands can hold and touch; that of the aromas we smell and the colours — not screen-bound — we see. It's a little like the Marxist blueprint: without hands, imaginary figures become so abstract as to lose meaning. The materialism that we lack is in no way theoretic — it is almost a contradiction in terms — but rather more tangible and, as such, the sincerest of them all. If we are not careful, then the digital era will be, first and foremost, the era of evasion, the new opium of the people. One might express it thus: 'Please, touch as much as you can'. Touch the earth, the tree trunks, stones, fruit, longed-for bodies, etc., caress the air and embrace your children and hold each other under blankets and prepare food for one another. Perhaps Heraclitus, sitting beside the fire, took a moment to grill a couple of sardines and toast a piece of bread, the pleasure of the first mouthful having been preceded by the aromas emitted by the fish and bread amongst the embers. This is the authentic materialism of things.

Simplicity does not mean banality. The true value of everyday life is not the product of a photography competition, nor is it necessarily aesthetic. That which fulfils the day to day, the passing of the months and years, might not be considered much, perhaps a kind of low, mediocre form of living that neither excels nor dazzles, a mute, 'materialistic' life, achieving little... And yet, this way of looking at things would be short-sighted. Not only because one could undertake an in-depth analysis of all excellences (fame, heroism, notoriety, honour, etc.) and find there much banality and false guises, but also because there is an unarguable dignity to be found in the simplicity of people's lives. Put it like this: does earning one's daily bread require less effort than creating art? Is the day-to-day labour of the baker, mechanic, carpenter or doctor baser than that of cultural creation? Mediocrity lies in all pretensions to excellence that, despite everything, remain chained to mere banality: ephemeral fame, snobbish theories, publicity and marketing, etc.

To the question: 'Which is the best way to live?', one might respond: a life dedicated to adventure or political life, as Arendt argued, or a contemplative life, as an important part of Greek and Christian tradition believed. Yet, at times, there is a kind of excellence that exists only when elitist: the idea that there will be those who carry out the 'baser' work, like slavery, for example. Fortunately, many of us have known a type of daily life that could be a candidate for 'the best way to live' and that, what's more, is in no way elitist. A certain satisfaction with one's ordinary life is within the reach of the majority of people, going against the logical current of property, power or fame. In effect, this non-elitist way of living doesn't run out because most people opt for it, while the others are logically exclusive: only a small minority can aspire to them as wealth, power and fame are always for minorities. And to that we might add another decisive difference: the ethics of an ordinary life are not ethics of appearance, while power, wealth and glory are often sustained through mere appearances. This is condemned by the stoics, Augustine and Pascal, with all of them following the ever-present Socratic exhortation:

'Most excellent man, are you [...] not ashamed to care for the acquisition of wealth and for reputation and honour, when you neither care nor take thought for wisdom and truth and the perfection of your soul?'[6]

The logic of caring for one's spirit or soul is *democratic* or *popular* and is within everyone's reach. Let us, however, take a look at the logic of political action such as Arendt's concept that the only thing that can bring light to one's life is dignified public speech deserving of being remembered and that leads one directly to the distinction between the few and the many (who will not be remembered by anyone); and also that the classic model of contemplative life will flow into the monastic model of religious life. Specifically, the Protestant reformations brought about a critique of monastic vocation as a superior lifestyle from a religious point of view. In the same way that there is no special dedication for the Protestant, so there is no sacred place for excellence. In theory, in criticising the superiority of mediations and the mediations within them, the Protestant Reformation carries out a re-evaluation of ordinary life. As such, reflections on the monastic model in this essay in no way indicate the superiority of contemplative life, but rather show a way of everyday life in which contemplation is articulated with the, often, manual work of the day-to-day. Finally, neither can the value of artistic creation be doubted; this despite the fact that

6. Plato, *Apology of Socrates*, (tr. H.N. Fowler), Loeb, 1913

common sense is also an artist, and an accomplished one at that. And the apparently trivial daily gesture contains a strength that comes from very far away, enduring still thanks to this. If time is the strainer through which passes only true excellence, then the daily gesture sits right at the top of the list. It is the excellence of a wise, mysterious and artistic simplicity.

The simplicity of daily life sups from a most special, discrete wisdom linked to a gesture that is truly admirable and down which we slide in our desire to bring structure to it. In this vein, Jean François Billeter's wonderful essay, *Leçons sur Tchouang-tseu* (Lectures on Zhuangzi), is highly recommended. Focussing on what we do when doing something brings us closer to the supreme form of knowledge that exists in the gesture. Shepherd, butcher, locksmith, gardener, masseur, farmer... all are wise professions of a wisdom of gestures that have been shaped over the passing of the days and acquired experience.[7] No wisdom is improvised, nestled in the complicity of the glancing look between the shepherd and his sheepdog, the hammer upon the glowing iron, etc. The maturity of wisdom reveals itself when the gesture is entirely obedient to the thing. This cannot be called 'objectivism' (as objectivism consists of having distanced yourself from things). In the wisdom of the gesture, there is a continuity between the 'subjectivity' of the body and the 'thingness' of the thing. Understanding, obedience and a knack for something are all one. We call it *doing things well*. Everything lies in *the way of doing* things. To live by The Heavens, as Zhuangzi says, or following the will of God, according to some Christian writers; they both mean the same thing. Let us repeat: everything lies in the how. Look at this choice quote from Joseph Hall, an English bishop and writer in the first half of the 17th Century: 'God loveth

7. Here Joan Maragall's poem, 'Elogi del viure' is too apt not to cite at least the last few verses: *El món s'adobaria bé tot sol, | només que cadascú | fes el seu deure amb amor, | a casa seva* (*The world would alone be fertilised | if but each person | in their homes | would do their duty with love*)
Joan Maragall, 'Elogi del viure' [Eulogy to Life], (tr. translator's own)

adverbs'. We might also add here that the better part of life can be found in verbs and adverbs. Nor is there any need to take part in any post-modern, anti-substantialist offensive in order to support this assertion: simply remaining vigilant to experience is more than enough.

One aspect of this wisdom has been called *common sense*, the natural ally of daily life. It is called *common* because it is presumed to exist in everyone, but it could be called *everyday sense* as it is forged within each and every one of us through the serene passing of the days. And so, precisely because of this, because of its diachronic genesis, it guides us better than any other *sense*. It is not banal or over-pragmatic. It is also 'existentialist', knowing that every day is the last. As such, it values today and the next. If every day is like the last, we should care for what we have in front of us, a kind of *carpe diem* that is neither precipitated nor egocentric. Linking opportunity to the exceptional would be a mistake as, in doing so, frustration is almost certainly assured. No, it should be linked to the *day-to-day*.

And then, together with common sense, ordinary language. In the shadow of relentless nihilism, attention to ordinary language guides. Something that, on the other hand, is produced neither by the specialised languages of the new social and human sciences nor — despite their best efforts — from the omnipresent 'neuros' — neurolinguistics, neuro-ethics, neuro-politics, etc. The intentionally extreme philosophical exercises (such as *Metaphysical Meditations* by Descartes) find their counterpoint in normal life and common sense and the language that comes with it. It is a most adequate exercise, as long as the starting point is not underestimated. When this happens, and a kind of festering is produced in its abstraction, one should do what Wittgenstein says: '*We* redirect the words from their metaphysical usage towards a more daily use'. The movement can be easily picked up again in both senses, with the condition that in no way should the world of common sense — that is, in a terminology that has already been fixed solid by contemporary philosophy, the *Lebenswelt* ('The World of Life') — be forgotten, as this is nothing but the basis of everything. Familiar language, something that allows us to speak of that which we experience, is the starting point of all thought and creation. To be able to speak is to distance yourself from confusion and indifference, this first way out being if not categorical, then existential. The virtue of common sense consists of the fact that, requiring very little in exchange, it helps to correct the detours of abstract thought. This was explained very well by Mendelssohn through his exchanges with Lessing: 'Wherever reason distances itself from good common sense, or deviates and is in danger of taking a wrong turn, the philosopher will not believe his own arguments...' In contrast to overly contrived arguments and pedantic discourse, there should be: 'assertions and judgements from a common sense that is both simple and well-founded, contemplating things correctly and reflecting on them calmly'. The master, however, of the revindication of common sense is Franz Rosenzweig. Faced with the end of the philosophy that in some way represents the Hegelian answer to the question: 'What is everything?', and stating that 'everything' comes from the Absolute Spirit, Rosenzweig reclaims the wisdom of a healthy common sense; wisdom that recommends — as a remedy to the sickness of abstractions — a return to the waters of life from which we have all too adroitly distanced ourselves:

'As, in the end, one cannot deny daily life in favour of some sublime sentiments that would be much more 'authentic' than tough reality. Earthly hustle manages to impose itself. And with it once again life's natural articulation, the power of occurrences, precisely this force of daily life with its ever-renewed small labours and existing names.'[8]

8. Franz Rosenzweig, *Das Büchlein vom gesunden und kranken Menschenverstand* [*Understanding the Sick and the Healthy: A View of World, Man, and God*], (tr. translator's own)

Rosenzweig has been able to demonstrate that the curative capacity of common sense consists of taking both time — the occurrences of life — and proper nouns seriously. This recovery requires 'returning' to life and, as he states, the demands of the day. If we have distanced ourselves from life, it's because we are afraid of death. But death is unavoidable, regardless of our desires to stay it or our involvement in special projects such as submerging ourselves in an intemporal metaphysical meditation through which we arrive at the conclusion that, in the end, everything is One. Common sense knows that the principal truth is revealed every day. In other words, that the truth is to be found not in underlying depths or even in the underlying end. The truth is the truth of each thing, of each thing in its own time, and of the present that is given and taken away. It is because of this that there is danger in the act of staying still: stopping so as to open the door onto abstraction leads to despair because nothing comes of this intemporal pause, nothing manifests itself; one is locked up and falls ill. Indeed, Hell would be definitive imprisonment.[9] Desperation is also due to a certain type of imprisonment and there is nothing one can do except to 'get out' — literally — back to everyday life: 'You have to get out of here'. Likewise, illness is both imprisonment of the self and, in a way, the imprisonment of time (as if nothing will or can happen). To return to the day-to-day is to return to life. It is rediscovering the opportunity of the day-to-day, the demands and invitations. Here is the good fortune of being able to return to normality (in political terms, too: from an exceptional state to normality). To return to normality, return to daily life, is a blessing. And it implies the very

9. There is a popular folk tale that explains the difference between Heaven and Hell: in Hell there is a table with many plates of a variety of exquisite foods. The diners, however, have one hand tied to a very long fork while the other is bound to a very long knife. As such, when they pierce and cut the food, they are unable to get the food close to their mouths. A terrible torture. And in Heaven? What is Heaven like? Well, it's the same: a table heaving under delicious food at which the diners' hands are tied to the strange cutlery. The only difference is that here, in Heaven, each diner cuts and pierces the food before moving it over to the mouths of the other diners.

same: picking up one's path again and along with it a certain amount of confidence.

After having mentioned verbs and adverbs, it is now nouns that show themselves to be decisive in daily life, most importantly in people's names. Life flows, everything changes, and yet our names stay the same. If in colloquial language verbs and adverbs reveal the wisdom of the action, nouns owe themselves to and are candidates for proximity. There is a big difference between calling people generic titles and using their own name. Calling someone by their own name is like looking into their eyes: it is only possible to say one person's name or look in their eyes at a time. Nouns — along with all words that provide shelter, as we will see later — are the linguistic form of proximity.

Though common sense lies close to things that happen, it is most important when in the vicinity of the occurrence of the specific, unique other; though let us note just how difficult it is for philosophical and scientific discourse to deal with this occurrence.

As well as satisfying one's needs, there is a place in the day-to-day for work so as to earn a living. Elements of daily life exist that are not means, or even a means to an end, but rather that satisfy themselves. Because of this, daily life is both a path (in a directional sense), and a meaning (the meaning already present in life). It is life enjoying life. It is delight in the world, in food and drink, in sex and spectacle. There exists a kind of immersion without dissolution that allows one to be carried away to be found in the day-to-day. An emptiness is filled, satiated. Hunger is the void, and delight in things is the way to fill it. And, upon this delight is laid the symposium, the banquet, shared joy. There is a meaning to life in the day-to-day that, despite the great cracks in the heavens of 'values', fails to totally collapse. The lowercase — though no less important than the uppercase — shows a lot more stability in the face of possible nihilistic convulsions and earthquakes. Resistance, here, is the resistance of significance, of meaning. Our worldview might fall, but we will continue experiencing proximity and our connection with the other and living in the day-to-day. That which resists, is the meaning of proximity. And so, we are unwise to assimilate necessities with that of the lowest dimension of the human being (as Arendt does). Saving daily life from discredit means showing that food, weariness from working and the moment of rest, apart from their obvious links to necessity, are also a response to the abyss. That which is human doesn't wait to manifest itself in the superior regions of political action or contemplative thought; it already does it with the same intensity through the daily gesture. Hairs, therefore, must be split if we are to avoid running the risk of simplification. The most elemental things are intrinsically able to respond to or resist the darkness and exposure. Nihilism, like finitude, cannot be overcome and so must be faced. We oscillate between proximity and the abyss, and proximity is a response to the abyss.

So, instead of seeing itself as a way of going further and beyond, the more explicitly thoughtful life can be understood as an attempt to return to proximity. However — and this is important — this is by way of a path (a reflection) that allows one to realise certain aspects that before dwelled in the shadows. And this reflection wouldn't be far removed from the daily gesture. Both aim to increase proximity with life. Thinking is a way of moving closer to the more primordial. And in this way, we are compelled to stop opposing daily gestures with an attitude of meditation. Both go in the same direction; they know — though in different ways — that the most profound can be found in that which is closest: in the dawn echoing creation, the first moment things come into the light; in work; in coffee or conversation to draw one closer to the other; in returning home, the beginning and end of all other returns; in the waiting and hoping that saturates every moment and without which life would be insufferable (our muscles would stiffen, our breathing accelerate, our breath would freeze); in our daydreams — an essential dose of distraction as demanded by life's tension; in all that we do when making or building; in the difficult moments; in the moments of satisfaction for all we have accomplished. And, just like that, a *confidence* emerges in the 'getting on with things' of the day-to-day.

V. A BRIEF MEDICAL MEDITATION

One of the most apparent and significant elements of our resistance is, without doubt, when we find ourselves in the face of illness. As such, doctors, along with teachers, are two most peculiar figures. Medicine and education are professions unlike the others: ignoring specialisation, they are commitments that all of philosophical anthropology would be wise to keep very much in mind. The *you* is both teacher and doctor, right from the primordial moment in which their presence is, in itself, both teaching and help. One can find the figures of doctor and teacher — or similar — in almost all cultures; likewise, one can provide a sociological description and justification for both. But before being sociological or cultural categories, teacher and doctor figures are — let's say — ontological, relative to the fundamental way of being a person. And so, what manner of relationship is there between these exceptional categories, between doctor and teacher, between medicine and philosophy?

The Greeks insisted that while medicine might enable one to understand how to cure the body, philosophy does the same but of the spirit. This idea deserves to be *reinitiated* which, in other words, means leaving the commonplace behind, rethinking the thing itself, and so emphasising the overlooked evidence.

Doctor means 'someone who *takes care* and *cures*' or, in other words, someone who cares and heals. *Medicine* and *remedy* comply with this. Obviously, the act of healing presupposes illness, the fact that the human being is vulnerable and threatened by injury and illness and subject to ageing. This meditative resetting of medicine and philosophy requires tackling the meanings of the act of curing, of health and of illness.

That the determination is ontological implies that, in some way, we are all doctors and philosophers. The fact that the sick are also cared for at home, and that there are 'homemade' remedies, is equivalent to the fact that, fortunately, both parents and friends are teachers, and that philosophical questions are not restricted to academic spheres, but spring up everywhere. But this doesn't mean there can't be a vocation, a talent and a dedication that make their acts more productive and effective: they are all the above, and it therefore means studying them without, however, detaching them from the more basic register from which they take their meaning.

THE CONDITION OF THE DOCTOR

A good example of the doctor's condition can be found in two characters from *The Plague*, Albert Camus' best known novel. One of them, of course, is Doctor Rieux, the protagonist and narrator of the events that happen in the still French-controlled North African city of Oran when, in the middle of the 20th Century, it is struck by a plague that is, as unlikely and anachronistic as it might seem, the very same that devastated Europe during the Medieval period. The epidemic — a metaphor in part for war and concentration camps — is an extreme occurrence that pushes the characters to the limit. Rieux, who like many doctors was a very busy man before the outbreak thanks to the demands of his job, laments and regrets having not dedicated enough time to his wife who, during the events of the novel, finds herself in a Swiss sanatorium, where she eventually dies. He is a good doctor: knowledgeable, experienced and humble when recognising his limits. At the beginning, when what is happening is still unclear, he puts all of the information he has been able to gather at the service of his colleagues. With a general stupefaction before the abnormality of the situation, the city authorities and a handful of doctors hold a meeting at the prefecture so as to decide what is to be done. All symptoms seem to suggest the plague. The politicians are nervous and indecisive. Rieux, on the other hand, while demonstrating his honesty by recognising the lack of certainty, recognises the necessity of acting 'as if' it were the plague because, rather than a medical thesis, human lives are on the line.

Throughout the epidemic, Rieux works to exhaustion every day, yet even then he tenaciously continues to try to find a solution. In the most unpleasant part of the book, he takes part in the production of a new vaccine, deciding to try it out on the Judge Othon's son, the administered medicine drawing out the boy's agony. Amidst the agony and pain, the doctor meets an old Jesuit called Peneloux in the boy's bedroom. Both of them have very different points of view on life, but they are in agreement when it most matters. Indeed, Rieux says to the priest: 'We are working together for something that unites us at a higher level than prayer or blasphemy, and that's all that counts.'[1]

Despite the failure, Rieux doesn't give up and, months later, will try a new serum, this time successfully, though his success fails to bring about any sense of scientific triumphalism in him. He knows that what counts are the people who still find themselves in a weakened state. This is why the medical vocation is much better explained in Camus' text than Plato's well-known *Laws*, with its doctor-teacher figure. The doctor is a person of action and study, tenacious and dedicated, insatiable, and convinced that their work has meaning. In fact, according to Plato's classification in *Laws*, Rieux would likely be the slave doctor who is said to have been literally running 'from one sick man to another'.[2] When, in the end, the plague is defeated and the city erupts in celebration, he knows full well that his work is not finished: 'His work went on: there is no holiday for the sick.'[3]

There is no need for grandiloquence or extraordinary, almost mystical, vocations. It can all be a lot simpler. When asked by a friend, Rieux remembers why he had decided to become a doctor:

1. Albert Camus, *The Plague*, (tr. R. Buss), Penguin, 2020
2. *Ibid.*
3. *Ibid.*

'When I first took up this profession, I did so in a sense abstractedly, because I needed to, because it was a career like another, one of those that young people consider for themselves. And, perhaps, also because it was especially hard for someone like myself, a working man's son. And then I had to see people die.'[4]

His work leads him to experience something that he will never get used to: the fact that world order is governed by death, and one must fight back against it. Human beings must never get used to it, as it is here that habit, if it means drying out, undermines us. The very worst tragedy lies in the act of getting used to tragedy.

Medicine is *resistance* in the face of the offensive of sickness. And from here comes the appropriateness of the anthropological concept of resistance in all of its forms. It is because of this that in Camus' text, the profile of medical responsibility does not manifest itself only in doctor Rieux. There is another character who, defined as such, is just as or even more important. This is Tarrou, a man who had everything in the first epoch of his life — good health, success, and no serious worries: 'When I was young I lived with the idea of my innocence; that is to say, with no idea at all. Yet one day I started thinking…', and honest reflection leads to shame or, in other words, consciousness:

'With time I have simply noticed that even those who are better than the rest cannot avoid killing or letting others be killed because it is in the logic of how they live and we cannot make a gesture in this world without taking the risk of bringing death. Yes, I have continued to feel ashamed, and I learned that we are all in the plague, and I have lost my peace of mind.'[5]

That shame is the origin of philosophy would be one of the priceless Levinasian theses. From understanding — which

4. *Ibid.*
5. *Ibid.*

is essentially the understanding of responsibility or, in other words, of the act of being responsible — Tarrou extracts a kind of imperative which well defines the figure of the authentic doctor:

'Of course, there should be a third category, that of the true healers, but it's a fact that one does not meet many of those, because it must be hard to achieve. This is why I decided to place myself on the side of the victims, on every occasion, to limit the damage. Among them, I can at least seek how one arrives at the third category, that is to say at peace.'[6]

Here, the authentic doctor is defined as someone who places themselves at the service of others so as to help them. Doctor, nurse, aid worker… they are all names of the same profile, of the same way of being. Tarrou sets to work tirelessly for the health organisations against the spread of the epidemic, eventually losing his life.

THE DOCTOR AS THE NURSE, THE NURSE AS THE DOCTOR

Illness or injury makes us get weaker, feebler, at times not able to stand. This common experience is what leads to the meaning of the word *nurse* (coming from Middle English *nurshen, norishen* 'to supply with food and drink, feed; bring up, nurture'). A nurse is dedicated to *bringing up*, to helping the *infirm* stand up again.

As we all know, in order to be strong, we need to eat. It is in no way a coincidence that the most common question in situations of illness is the ever typical: 'Is he/she eating?' Food nourishes both the body and the spirit and is a source of strength. As such, that our word *nurse* should come from the Latin *nutrire*, or *nourish*, speaks volumes.

The nurse is a person who, so as to make them stronger, cares

6. *Ibid.*

for and nourishes — and, if needs be, feeds — those who for some reason find themselves frail, weak and bedbound. Indeed, the root for the word *clinic* is related to the Greek for *bed* and *to lie*. The nurse is on vigil, like a guard on watch. It is significant that, in this field, one of the most emblematic references is Florence Nightingale, a 19th Century British nurse known as 'The Lady of the Lamp' due to the fact that she would go around the hospital beds every night with a lamp in her hand to see if any of the poor prostrated patients needed anything. Just the lone light of the lamp or candle help to distance the sick from the anxieties and fears of the night. And the gently whispered: 'good night' has the same effect as the lamp: it illuminates and calms.

All houses serve to recover strength, but some in a more specific way. Almshouses or Charity Houses, Old People's Homes, etc., were once specifically intended for the weakest of us: orphans, the elderly and the sick. The most common name for a place where sick people are treated is *hospital*. An exceptionally vivid figure in this sense is that of Juan de Granada — Joan de Déu — who would walk the city streets looking for desperate poverty and disease-stricken people in porchways before hauling these people up onto his back and taking them to the hospital that he himself had opened. The nurse and doctor are facets or parts of the same activity. Taking in weakness so as to renew strength, or sickness so as to recuperate health: this is the idea of the hospital and the doctor-nurse activity that takes place there. Vocation and dedication that, most correctly, Florence Nightingale called: 'The most beautiful of all the fine arts.' Its excellence comes from its being an art that implies an interpersonal relationship. It is technique and dialogue, art and relation, procedure and contact, method and treatment, all at the same time. Noble on two fronts: firstly because it is only service to the weakest that leads to peace and, secondly, because it puts into perspective that which contemporary culture — without having been able to fully understand the illustrated discourse of autonomy — has discarded all too rapidly: mutual dependence. Nobody stands alone. We provide mutual support (though at times we need more in especially difficult situations). Personal strength depends on others — on their recognition, on their welcoming embrace — and it's because of this that reducing the relationship between autonomy and dependency to a simple conflict is an error.

When the protagonist falls ill in Tolstoy's well-known, almost autobiographical novel, *The Death of Ivan Ilyich*, the characters around him — his wife, the majority of his children, his acquaintances, etc — all demonstrate their lack of scruples. All except for one secondary character who is the only one to truly — physically and emotionally — help Ivan Ilyich. He is Gerasim, a young butler in the service of the family. Of poor farming origins, he carries out the lowliest of jobs, but his constant positivity moves Ivan. Requiring this positivity more and more, Ivan leans on both the boy's physical strength as well as his strength of character, which comes not from culture or education but rather from his virtue and sincerity. In an obvious and very literal way, Gerasim represents the figure of the nurse.

VERTICALITY, COSMICITY, HEALTH AND ILLNESS

There exist apparently brilliant, though incorrect, phrases. There is a moment in which Hans Castorp, the main character in *The Magic Mountain*, reflects on his thoughts in the following way: '[…] the disease was a perverse, dissolute form of life. And life? Life itself? Was it perhaps only an infection, a sickening of matter?'[7] The idea that life could be an infection or sickening of matter can be found in more than one place. Does it mean to show the exceptionality or rarity of life? Let's do this another,

7. Thomas Mann, *The Magic Mountain*, (tr. H. T. Lowe-Porter), Vintage, 1992

better, way, whilst never going against what we understand by common sense, even if the result is less striking.

The wise old equation could be more or less reproduced in the following way: verticality is the expression of vitality, of life, of health. Strength is the condition of verticality. And cosmicity is the condition of strength. Disease — *and infirmity* — are the provisional or definitive loss of cosmicity and strength. In this equation, excluding medical activity, there remain many of the fundamental elements of this matter: verticality = life = cosmicity = health ≠ disease = instability = prostration.

The link between life and verticality can be demonstrated with the image of the tree of life. The verticality of the tree, stable enough to resist the wind, is an indication of strength ('Like the tree, we are beings to whom confusing forces come lie at one's feet')[8], of growth, of stability (both physical and moral) and, according to Bachelard, also of imaginative capacity. Let us also look, then, at the fact that one's signature — the Latin *signare* means to set a *mark upon, mark out, designate* — is the use of one's own name to affirm or strengthen something. It is only when someone cannot vouch for themself, when he or she is not sufficiently strong, that they require someone else to sign, affirm and respond for them.

Cosmicity is a concept the meaning of which brings together, with nuances, that which is indicated through the terms *harmony, balance, justice* and *orderliness*. A *cosmic* thing or situation is precisely that which produces good harmony and a certain completeness. *Cosmic* is the antonym of *chaotic, untidy,* and *unbalanced*. That cosmicity is the basis of verticality means that verticality in this sense has nothing to do with rigidity and hardness but rather a verticality that is both flexible and fragile. As such, for example, moral strength is more closely linked to *epikeia* and adaptability than rigorousness and immobility. Finally, the states of verticality and the cosmicity of the body are identified

8. Gaston Bachelard, *L'air et les songes*, [*Air and Dreams*], (tr. translator's own)

with its health. The Greek doctors insisted in this equivalence: health is harmony, and disease is its loss. But it is not a uniquely Greek notion. There are many diverse remedies, techniques and therapies in different cultures, and the equivalence of health and balance can be found in the majority of them.

Each of us is a cosmicity, not a mere conglomeration of organs, functions, and capacities. This cosmic *all* is an *opening*, and we call this opening the *world*. That which we often call *mental illness* demonstrates this circumstance: mental health is a state of balance that allows a good opening; a good way of experiencing the world. Mental illness, on the other hand, is a lack of equilibrium that restricts or annuls this relationship. People often say that a person is 'a little unbalanced' when it is clear that a person lacks good relationships with others, with themselves, and with other things. To say, therefore, 'open cosmicity' is redundant. Human cosmicity is unique in everyone, genderless. It is a condition of taking charge of one's own life, of purposefully assuming control. Human cosmicity: something that I will later call *conjunction*.

When one is fine, one's own cosmicity, especially in corporal terms, goes unnoticed. It's when one is unsettled that one becomes more aware of that which was once there before. This also explains what is meant by a kind of ontological priority given to being healthy over being ill. The condition of disease is health. What's more, this ontological priority also explains — or if not, links to — the religious hope of 'salvation', of health.

Disease reminds us of our mortal destiny. We move within the tension between the ontological priority of health — and the experience of health — and the experience of disease and the awareness of death. Indeed, while disease is something strange and disturbing, health (and life) is a 'miracle'. Human cosmicity is a marvellous, impenetrable mystery while weakness, frailty, and discomfort are all effects of disease. As we have already said: not only physical frailty, but also mental, moral weakness. Disease is the loss of cosmicity, it is imbalance and so, in an absolutely elemental sense, *disease is injustice*. Confusion often comes from the idea of the 'natural nature' of disease, as a disease can be both natural and unjust. And while *unjust* has an almost physical and topological meaning, it rapidly becomes moral and political. Disease is unjust because it unbalances; disease is unjust because of its disproportion (there are worse diseases than others); disease is unjust because of the inequality of its effects ('it never rains, but pours').

Despite the social conditioning of many diseases, it is clear that there is a 'naturalness' of disease that requires us not to distort the concept of nature and that demands the admittance of conflict that exists at times between a naturalness of what is given and human cosmicity. In a certain sense, human cosmicity can be considered as given. But it can also be lost 'naturally'. And it can be recuperated. And it is precisely within this possibility that the role of medical activity lies.

Medical activity can be defined as a cure by which to maintain cosmicity (with the determination of healthy life habits) and the effort so as to recuperate it when it has been affected by the entropic and degenerative causes brought on by disease. Medical activity is the protection of health, resistance in the face of the incursion of pathogens and the curing of wounds or imbalance. Obviously, in all of this, to medical activity can be added another, altogether more decisive factor: the spirit of the sick person and the forces that operate within them.

WHEN CARING TEACHES US TO THINK

Let's go back to the beginning of this chapter. What can philosophy relearn from medicine? What is the relationship between doctor and teacher? What can these vocations tell us of the human situation?

The New Testament makes reference to the phrase: 'Physician, heal thyself!'[9] that Nietzsche repeats in *Thus Spoke Zarathustra*: 'Physician, help yourself: thus also you help your sick'.[10] The reason for this is that both doctor and teacher affect others, not only through applied techniques and taught contents, but also through a kind of diffusing glow. While the sophist cares not for their students, rather instructing and occasionally enlightening them, the philosopher does, due to the fact that the cosmicity of their spirit configures yet more cosmicity. Cosmicity radiates out and is contagious, less in the sense of a tangible, plastic shape in which one can see themselves mirrored, and more in the sense of radial affectation. And it's precisely due to this glowing that *proximity becomes teaching*. A good teacher is also a doctor, firstly because they take care of their disciples and, later, because the atmosphere around them is beneficial. Contrarily, rhetoric is always cold and *indistant*.

We talk about *medical assistance* and *medical attention*, though both assistance and attention are, in themselves, already medical. To assist means staying at someone's or something's side. As does the act of attending to someone or something. Already being at someone's side is the modest *soil* offered to the other. Confidence and care are both initiated in the presence of proximity. As such, in terms of what the essence of medicine and the doctor's vocation do, the fundamental ethical value comes from the same place. Medicine and ethics respond to the same sense of humanity: to attend to those in need. Rather than getting too carried away with the creation of new deontological codes, what is truly decisive is not losing the radical sense of medicine.

Doctor, nurse, aid worker... they are different forms of the same gesture of resistance in the face of the entropic forces that attack and lay siege to human life. This gesture doesn't require any justification; rather it's the act itself that can be used as a kind

9. Luke 4:23, New Revised Standard Version
10. Friedrich Nietzsche, *Thus Spoke Zarathustra*, (tr. A. del Caro), CUP, 2006

of posterior justification. It is a human gesture *par excellence*, and the start of any justification.

Perhaps it's because of this that we should pay great attention to any deviations. We wouldn't want — through 'good (yet disorientated) intentions' — to lose the strength of this crucial resistance, of which we never have enough. One of these deviations is the current *pathologicalisation and medicalisation of life*. In other words, the tendency to consider every problem as a health problem (through which 'new diseases' are generated), thus prioritising pharmaceutical and, eventually, surgical treatments instead of placing more emphasis on public health policies that promote healthy lifestyles while enabling a more sensible understanding of the human condition. A reflection of this problem can even be identified in the World Health Organisation's definition of *health*: 'A state of total physical, mental and social wellbeing'. Taken directly from their literature, this can never be achieved and so, therefore, everyone is ill. To the restlessness and disorientation of modern humans can be added this unfortunate definition of health, so all-encompassing that one will always be able to find more than one motive to feel ill and so visit the doctor. Maximalisations often frustrate and this definition of health makes us all ill.

VI. CARING FOR YOURSELF WITHOUT BECOMING NARCISSUS

CARE OF THE SELF

Intimate resistance can be negatively expressed as a *not giving up* in the face of disintegrating forces and threats. To not give up, to not let anything be lost, to not allow that which we guard to be taken. This can even be taken to the extreme, to the very point when all hope seems lost. What lesson can we take from this experience? How is it that humans are capable of this kind of strength? Especially when it is easier — and, for this very reason, more usual — to adjust to the facts (if they are pleasurable) or give in to fatalism (if the facts are painful), why is there this determination to 'get on with things' and stay true to oneself?

Socratic tradition, clearly distinguishing it from any kind of narcissism, has called this 'getting on with things' the *care of the spirit* or *care of the self*. Resistance would only be narcissistic were it to focus solely on the self; but care for the other is inherent to resistance. The absurd is Narcissus's loneliness. In fact, etymologically, *absurd* comes from 'deaf, dull, mute' and so relates to someone who is out of tune or says things that don't make any sense due to their isolation from the exterior. Nowadays — as has been said more than once — degeneration represented by the therapeutic psychologist contributes to the deafness of the absurd. Very easy to detect, it needs only to be accompanied by the rhetoric of self-improvement. Meanwhile, some radical life experiences continue, as ever, to place us in situations requiring us to face up to things, in situations of repetition (but not of overcoming). Finitude and death cannot be overcome. Rather, they are faced. This, as simple as it is fundamental, is purposefully ignored by 'therapeutical restlessness' as it blends the rhetoric of personal realisation with methods supposedly based on holistic knowledge coming from all manner of sources.

Ignorance of finitude is ignorance of oneself, hidden away and damaged by an inflated ego. While its use might already have inferred its meaning, it's worth going over the distinction between *oneself* and *the self*. At times, we can relate *the self* (and similar expressions) to impersonality (the self that follows that which is said or done), but this goes hand in hand with egoism as the inflated ego involves itself in impersonal movements such as possession, mimicry and navel-gazing. On the other hand, experience of *oneself* presents itself not as either impersonal or egotistical, but rather through solitude and worry for the other. It is an experience of one's own 'exposure' and a solicitation to the vulnerability of one's fellow being

Many different things have been said regarding the reflection of one's own self. Augustinian tradition stands out as having situated the truth and path towards God in 'the interior': '*Noli foras ire, in te ipsum redi; in interiore homine habitat veritas*' ('Do not wander far and wide but return into yourself. Deep within man there dwells the truth'). According to this tradition, deep within each of us we would discover a kind of light (that, perhaps weaker today, remains the most mysterious light of them all) that would not only illuminate us but indicate the heights to which we aspire. Yet one would have to split hairs so as not to confuse Augustinian intuition with more clearly agnostic ideas such as not equating — as we have mentioned — gazing inwards with narcissistic tendencies. When this happens or, in other words, when the isolated self starts navel-gazing, nothing is to be found except for what C.S. Lewis called: 'hatred, loneliness, despair, rage, ruin and decay'. Nor is it necessary to be as anti-secular as *The Chronicles of Narnia* author was in order to share this opinion. Narcissus experiences nothing because he is isolated and, as such, has no escape route (no life). Specifically, Narcissus has no experience of his own misery, of his nothingness, and so is trapped and suffocated by his own image. As such, we learn yet again that there is no access to anything higher without the experience of nothingness.

So then, there are various motives for contrasting *oneself* and *the self*, and for placing closure, impersonality and egoism as possible manifestations of *the self* while, on the other hand, reserving that which is most highly valued of all for *oneself*: interior dialogue, responsibility, strength, freedom, one's own name, etc. This explains how, when reflecting, the sharpest of authors can write such different things: they are not dealing with the same aspects and so there is no need to oppose judgements like those of Luther and Pascal. According to Luther, man is a twisted wood that is bent over and into itself and that there is no way of straightening it out (this is egoism). Opposingly, for Pascal, we are extroverted and are, therefore, banal and prone to losing ourselves; prayer is one of the ways — one of the curves — that leads one to oneself. The egoism detected by Luther and the dispersion highlighted by Pascal are not all that different to one another, and both contrast with that which is more appropriate — Luther's awareness of one's own nothingness and Pascal's seclusion.

But *to reflect is to care for oneself*. In fact, it is through reflection that *oneself* emerges. Reflection is not introspection, if by *introspection* we understand a manner of searching within the interior of the self. Is the self an interior with contents? What happens more often than not is that reflection — a flexion on oneself — is rather a reflection of one's own experience. And here lies the best of contemporary existentialist considerations: a displacement of the abstract self for the movement of existence, and reflection on the contents of the consciousness for reflection on the experience of life. And so it is through this reflection that we find ourselves speaking of the emergence of *oneself* and of the place where resistance and proximity become clear.

Oneself appears suddenly as each of us experiences ourselves as something that happens, as an occurrence. I might glimpse my son's depths before he does, but I will never 'feel' it in the same way that he will. It is one thing to be born, when as individuals we come into the world, and another when *oneself* appears as a kind of trauma: one day we see ourselves truly and absolutely alone and we know that there is nothing we can do about it. In fact, we later start doubting our desire to do anything about it, though it is impossible to imagine how this might be possible. We see that the life of *oneself* is not so much a circle but rather a straight line that takes us from and towards the unknown. The experience of oneself also recognises the entirely opportune nature of having our own name, recognising that what is important — what is most essential — will never be gender in terms of gender, or even the lack of determination of a physical or metaphysical plan. No *apeiron* from which emerge all determinations and into which they all end up being diluted. This is why, through this occurrence of *oneself*, we must consider Deleuze's idea — though excellent — to be completely out of place, especially as it is illustrated in one of his last pieces of work, 'L'immanence: une vie...' [*Pure Immanence*], in which he compares the life of a specific person with a life: a mere life already inclined towards the impersonal movement of life, without the individuality or personal names linked to the self. Differentiating between 'the life' and 'a life', Deleuze says that 'a life' tends to be a type of basic deindividualization. 'The life' is a type of opposition to 'a life', as if 'the life' were positioned above 'a life', the second 'life' being the truly profound one. In order to illustrate this, Deleuze alludes to the figures of the newborn — it is said that all newborn babies look similar — and the dying. And he quotes a scene from Charles Dickens' novel, *Our Mutual Friend*, in which a group of people feel pity for a brigand because he is dying and is nothing more than *a life* that is fading away and extinguishing. But then the dying man suddenly gets a little better and comes back to life. And so, in being once again one with their life, he suffers the rejection from those who just a moment before were lamenting him. Those who were lamenting *a* life, now reject *the* life of this person. To me, this idea doesn't work. Old age might be interpreted as the weakening of the individual in terms of the body and strength but, despite this, it still supposes a stronger presence of *oneself*. Life experience places us in the paradoxical situation of the self. It is traumatic and yet, despite this, a mysterious and highly valued depth. What is sobering, what is truly important, is not the impersonal movement of life, but rather each and every singular and unique life.

The empire of reification is — as they unceasingly repeated at the Frankfurt School in the early 20th Century — the obstacle placed upon the experience of *oneself*. And still we continue under the same siege, reinforced three-fold by a scientific divulgation that started badly and ended up even worse; by a new screen-based fascination and a pathological consumer-centric self. It is a thin exterior and a weak interior stuffed with grandiloquence leading to a lesser life experience. Because of this we tell ourselves all manner of anecdotes and stories while we skimp on the transmission of the experience. Superficial shocks or pleasurable, fleeting life lessons are sooner mentioned, but experience is a daily transmission that is constantly narrated: that of the elderly person to the youth, or the teacher to the apprentice, or an extermination camp survivor to the new generation... Experience can have a prolonged character over time — 'one can gain experience' — until ripening like a fruit. Or one might also have a more enclosed yet radical and disruptive experience. In both cases, experience implies a *metanoia*, a change in the way of existing within the world and understanding life. Here, for example, nihilism is a most misunderstood denomination, because it can indicate a kind of superficial atmosphere of disbelief or can be — as we have demonstrated — the name of an experience. In the second case, it might seem to be a poisonous cup to be avoided. On the contrary, it should be scoured. The current illness or disappearance of the experience is not so much a consequence of nihilism but rather its artificial softening that, paradoxically, leads to submission to new dogmas. On the other hand, to stare into nothingness intensifies the experience of life and the return to proximity.

We need to consider *intimate resistance* as a name for an *experience* belonging to the realm of *proximity*; a realm that cannot be visited fleetingly, but rather a place to inhabit. These days, remaining in this realm is not easy. It is not measured in metres or centimetres, and its opposite is not distance, but rather the ubiquitous monochrome of a technology-ridden world. We have seen how daily life and the gesture of the home are crucial forms of the experience of proximity. To this we can now add the care of the self which is careful, thoughtful reflection as ways of returning to the primordial. The vocation of thought is also urgent in today's world. Heidegger, too, talks of this movement of thought towards proximity in his well-known text *Discourse on Thinking* (*Gelassenheit*). In this, the German master represents a dialogue between three characters who, towards the end, agree that it was specifically proximity that they were looking for throughout their walk through the country. We notice that serenity produces proximity in the same way that the night brings out the stars. Observe: it is not that the *serene* night 'objectively' brings the stars closer, reducing or overcoming the enormous distances that separate them from us. The astronomical distances between the stars negate the need to talk of distance as distance is an indication belonging to the human world. Night, therefore, brings the stars closer by grouping them together and showing them to us; they come closer to each other, just as we move closer to them. This is how the serene night draws close; it is the path towards proximity. In other words, it's not by treating the stars as objects of scientific study that they draw near to us, but rather when, grouped together in the heavens, we treat them as those things that, night after night, accompany us on our fleeting mortal journey through existence.

To think is an experience because it doesn't leave things as they were. To think places one on a transformative personal path. Not only at the end of the path, but already halfway along, one is no longer who one was. To think is to reflect: to look within, towards the primordiality of life, thus resulting in transformation and conversion. The excellence of every great thinker comes from their own particular way of understanding and travelling along this path. Foucault, for example, speaks of his experience of thinking, concurrently seeing that thought has to be critical of everything that — like power — erodes and impoverishes the experience. His criticism of power (and all of its institutional tapestry) seeks not only to denounce forms of control and domination, but also the experience itself (not pure or unconditional, but still more intense, harder, even 'stranger', more unsettling) and, as such, other possible truths that might be extrapolated from this. And so, to write — itself a thought exercise — is an experience to which we might add some of Foucault's words:

'I don't always think exactly the same because my books are my experiences, in the most complete possible sense. An experience is something from which everyone comes away transformed. If I had to write a book so as to communicate that which I thought before writing it, I would never have the courage to start.'[1]

Experience transforms, both individually and collectively. The Foucaultian genealogy of the modern subject aims, therefore, to answer this question: 'How have we ended up being who we are?' But here we have the same intent at comprehension that experiencing something implies. The intent at comprehension, when removed from mere amateurism and exhibition, is that which the ancients called *ascesi*: an exercise about oneself from which one emerges transformed. And so it is that philosophy represents the care of the self: because what transforms is the exercise of thought.

1. Michel Foucault, *Dits et écrits*, [*Sayings and Writings*] (tr. translator's own)

It's not so much the act of thinking differently as it is to simply think. Because of this, it is neither easy nor habitual. Not only is it that the context little compels one to do it, but that it is often not even considered. This is a most unheard-of experience of what is often 'to think'. It requires seclusion and interior dialogue. As old Epictet said: 'Man, if you are someone, go and walk alone, talk with yourself, don't hide away within a chorus.' We have already said that solitude is not isolation. Solitude and company go together, both opposing massification and the herd; many groups are nothing more than forms of mass, and so it is important to discern the difference. There is, for example, the silence of the masses (masses can be both silent and noisy) and the silence of solitude or of company. And both silences are very different. That of the masses is deaf silence, while that of solitude and company is silence that allows words to come to the fore and thought to occur. That solitude is not isolation is demonstrated in the sense that its silence teaches us to listen and places us before the evidence emphasised by Zeno of Elea: 'Remember that nature has given us two ears and one sole mouth so as to teach us that it is more important to listen than to speak.'

Is interior dialogue not dialogue with another? And isn't it a preface of dialogue with others as fellow beings? Regarding dialogue, the other is neither a compliment nor excuse. It is not that which is necessary for dialectic discussion, or a piece to be integrated. The personal way of caring for the other is by welcoming. We were born to welcome one another (and the miserable immensity of dominance and violence has not demonstrated otherwise). Company is welcoming:

'Some old men came to see Abba Poemen and said to him: "When we see brothers who are dozing at the synaxis, shall we rouse them so that they will be watchful?" He said to them: "For my part when I see a brother who is dozing, I put his head on my knees and let him rest."'[2]

2. Anon. *The Saying of The Desert Fathers*, (tr. B. Ward), 1975

Even now, in some orthodox monasteries on Mount Athos, a monk goes once a day to find his spiritual father to explain the thoughts or desires he has had throughout the day. The monk is not looking for absolution or forgiveness, but simply a welcome and understanding. Often, the spiritual father does nothing more than bless him before sending him on his way. A warm welcome, already present in this gaze and gesture, makes the rest unnecessary. Indeed, the frankness of the welcome is the best encouragement that the welcomed person could hope to get. There is no need for well-educated people, but simply those with experience. They are to be recognised not by their affected, paternalistic and honeyed speech, but by their goodness, their respect and the humility they show to the other. Saint Benedict understood it perfectly: the aesthetic itinerary leads to the 'ineffable sweetness of love'.

ONESELF AS FREEDOM

Sartre says that freedom is like a prison sentence. Were we to continue with the metaphor, then we would have to add, however, that the sentence itself is also ambiguous: bitter and sweet; pleasurable and disturbing; serene and abysmal. Freedom is both a *condition* (this ambivalent condemnation) and an *aspiration*. In other words, it is a fundamental trait of the human condition (to think of freedom is to think of the human), and the most highly considered personal and political value (producing all of the innumerable individual and collective struggles for *liberation*). What is surprising is that the successive, particularly necessary, highly valued, and celebrated acts of liberation don't always lead to freedom as achieving the condition — as our society most worryingly demonstrates.

At times, freedom is defined as *self-determination*, an act to self-determine yourself within the social and political natural order. Then it is distinguished between the self-determination of action (freedom of action) and the self-determination of will (free will). Slavery, totalitarian regimes or imprisonment are situations that annul or diminish the freedom of action just as the effect of drugs or foolishness threaten free will. Oneself is that which within this traditional distinction is defined as *free will* and it is in the name that our existence manifests itself as capable of want and 'voluntary' aspirations. This capacity can be strengthened or, on the contrary, lost. *Insanity* has been understood as one of these states in which oneself has been lost, trapped within a cursed labyrinth, constantly reminding us of the fragility of oneself.

To approach oneself as a freedom (as free will or choice) allows us, in an indirect way, to recuperate the interpretive fruitfulness of the category of resistance. Let's start off by focussing on a colloquial expression. We can say: 'This person has been locked away for two years and is now *out on conditional bail*'. Within this phrase we understand that the conditional (or conditioned) freedom is not total freedom; rather it is a kind of semi-freedom. There are restrictions (related to the places where this person can go, certain obligations they have to comply with, etc.) that mean that freedom is not total. The person will only be free once all the conditions have been lifted and only then will the conditional regime allow *normal* life. So, while we might say that human freedom is conditional freedom, it is not in the sense that we've just explained as *it is not partial freedom due to conditions*. So as to better focus the question, we should think solely of *human freedom*, leaving to one side the abstract idea of 'freedom' as that which concerns us and about which we might say something is specifically *human freedom*. Through this, we quickly discover that while human freedom is a conditioned freedom, it is not that it's less free, but rather the opposite: it is more free precisely because it is conditioned. When we want to refer to the human being, it seems pertinent to use the words *human condition*, and while it's clear that by using this denomination we are not trying to indicate a restriction on the human being, the idea clearly contains limits. In this case, for example, limitation comes from our corporeality. Our bodies have their limits and some things they *can* do, and some things they *can't*: for example, in general, everyone can walk while nobody can fly without the help of some device. Corporeality is also linked to spatial and temporal limitations: we are not able to instantaneously move from one place to another or occupy a space already occupied by another compact object, we are unable to do many things at the same time, and we cannot travel backwards in time to yesterday, etc. There are also limits related to our knowledge and capacity to understand as well as limits related to our collective lives (for this to be possible we require rules and laws to keep it constant), etc. Yet none of this should be solely understood as a simple loss or decrease of our possibilities. The truth is that all of *these limitations are, at the same time, conditions of possibility.* In other words, they are things that open the door to our most personal possibilities. The well-known image of the pigeon used by Kant in his introduction to his *Critique of Pure Reason* is always useful when explaining this idea. The pigeon, says Kant, when wanting to fly freely and feeling the air resistance against its wings, might imagine that it would fly better within a vacuum. The truth is, though, that flying inside a vacuum is impossible. The pigeon might consider that the air slows down its flight a little but, on the other hand, it would not see that what slows it down is simultaneously that which allows it to fly; that that which slows it down is also the condition of possibility. This is the apparent contradiction and, in a way, the marvel: that which is resistance or limit is at the same time the condition of possibility. Human freedom — a freedom that is eminently conditioned — has to be understood from this condition: the limits of the human condition are the very same human condition that opens the horizon up to that which is possible. It might even be necessary to speak of it in these terms: *thanks* to our corporeal condition…; *thanks* to our social condition… With this in mind, analysis of certain things might well be more lucid. Because of this, for example, one might greatly eulogise the effort of political liberalism for the recognition of the liberty of all individuals faced with any kind of slavery and arbitrary control leading to the assumption that, as is often said, 'my freedom ends where others' starts'. Though without invalidating this, if one scratches at the surface a little, one arrives at something that is seemingly almost the opposite. Instead of being a restriction on my desires, others now reveal themselves as the condition of this want; I am with others and others make my freedom possible. Within this register can be seen that I am not with others *to use them* and that others, for me, are not a way of achieving an objective, but rather that I am *with* and *for the others*; mine is a social condition. I live with others in the same way that I live by breathing. Seen in this way, the social dimension is not so much an obstacle or even a limit on my freedoms, but rather its condition.

Oneself as freedom is, as Arendt would say, the introduction of novelty into the world, a beginning; the foundation of our uniqueness and of a suitable personal name. Everyone has an independent voice and everyone exists as oneself. It's because of this that the manifestation of each of our freedoms diminishes when impersonal regimes or atmospheres prevail; with the *it is said* or the *it is done*. But that which should now be underlined is that the plenitude and freedom of oneself is due to the condition of the other. Mounier speaks of this as *freedom as responsibility* and Levinas, *invested freedom*. Neither the primordial nor the plenitude of freedom are the act of the affirmation of the self, but rather the adequate correspondence with the condition. In other words, the recognition of the fortunate bond, the recognition of that which *frees the freedom* of its own affirmation. Oneself is the conquest of freed freedom, of the freedom granted from its own radical responsibility. As Levinas would say, the expressions of freedom are not so much the *here you have me* or *see me here*. The subject recognises its own condition of *being subjected*.

It is uncovered responsibility, especially when one approaches it and realises that they themselves are already penetrated, happily bound, and subjected by it. As if the 'I' getting closer, realised — now much clearer — that I have to respond to and for the other. Neighbourliness, together and with the same radicality, is both refuge and responsibility. As such, *absolute liberty* is an expression that, apart from being confusing, refers to anything that has little to desire. We are involved intimacy (luckily, 'summoned' in a most profound way); an intimacy that is configured through others, while not being reduced by them. We cannot distance ourselves from siblings without fault, indifference or egoism. We cannot distance ourselves from them, though we are always a little — or very — late because the interpellation between myself and others is more primordial than any of my other impulses or projects. That the other is a sibling means just this: that I am bound to them by demand, by claim; and sleeplessness is the condition provoked in me by them. We owe it to Levinas for having defined psychism as insomnia.

In this sense, to return to oneself is not to return to the *conatus* of the substance, to the immaculate identity or to the starting point of all of my future domains. To return to oneself is to empty yourself, and therefore discover yourself as being exposed, captured (subjected and held responsible) passivity. Classical outlines opted to speak of the *heart*; these days, we speak of *consciousness*. In both cases we refer to our more intimate capacity to comprehend (want and love). And from here come the derivatives: *cordially* and *attentively*, in which the cognitive and emotional become one. The intention is identical: we refer to oneself with the same supposed intimate depth of the heart or conscience, imbibed in us from long before the beginning. In contrast, pride cares only about itself, while ignoring that which is its own essence. The proud person is so obsessed with themself that they prefer themself over everything and everyone. So much pride and so little decorum! As Gabriel Marcel says: 'not being available means being occupied by the self.' But we should deconstruct that a little: not being available means to be so occupied by the self that one doesn't know which is most personal, the heart, oneself.

STRENGTH

> When I shall have grown weak enough — it won't take very
> long — the most trifling worry will perhaps suffice to rout me.[3]

We find ourselves once again faced by an ambiguity. On the one hand, the main stoic intuition is this: if it is cared for, then the oneself becomes invincible, and no tyrant would be capable of assailing its bastion, forcing it to surrender. Yet on the other hand, as we have shown, oneself is vulnerable, threatened by insanity, threatened by a string of social and political homogenisations and threatened by myriad disintegrating and dissolving forces. From this juncture, it is necessary to understand the cardinality of strength. Within the mineral world, the hardness of a rock corresponds to the life force present in the vegetal and animal worlds: the strength by which the plant drives its roots into the ground and lifts its trunk into the air; the strength by which the animal chases after its prey until catching it. Despite all this, strength, which tradition has considered to be one of the four cardinal virtues, is not proportional to physical force as we find examples of it in slight, physically weak men and women. We are dealing with a different strength, often called 'strength of spirit', which is related to oneself. In the same way that a lorry might cross a solid bridge, so too can each of us lean on a

3. Franz Kafka, *The Diaries of Franz Kafka 1914-1923*, (tr. M. Greenberg & H. Arendt), London, 1949

97

strong person, someone who might instil confidence and security in others. Strength is also self-confidence. Strength of spirit doesn't seek out victories about which to sing: it's discreet. Those who have it, do not flaunt it. The strong person recognises their weaknesses, just as the wise person recognises their ignorance. You can see where this is headed: here, awareness of weakness provides still more strength. Strength is not expressed through heroism or daring, but rather through stability, faithfulness and perseverance. It doesn't stand out, but provides confidence to those close by, embraces and helps. It is not public virtue, though even less so private. It is the sign of a profound spiritual life and of a great spirit. Magnanimity can be noted in its face, though not because it is intended, but simply because 'it's obvious'.

Strength is like a gear made up of two cogs: one is for supporting, while the other is for undertaking. In effect, strength is the capacity one has for enduring, for resisting and for putting up with adversity that *comes*. In this sense, patience, resistance and strength are one and the same. The second dented cog is related to one's capacity for taking things on, for starting up, or starting again. How can one start anything without having previously endured? How would one be in the condition to take on any kind of action without being able to tolerate all that weakens and discourages? As *to endure* is the condition that makes all posterior acts possible, unsurprisingly it's the most important part. More than anything, strength is the virtue of endurance. What's more, what happens is that if the action can be seen as something often specific, the resistance of strength is almost always a wall that requires perseverance and continuous effort. To persevere means just this: to stay firm where necessary. The scaffolding of any structure must not be allowed to fail at any time if the whole is to remain stable. The diminution of an organism's 'defences' is the supposed crack through which pathogens might perpetrate the assault. It's obvious that strength has nothing to do with passiveness or conservatism, rather the contrary: nothing is more fertile and capable of changing things; and it has nothing to do with recklessness, which is notable in its blindness and disproportion.

Strength as resistance before adversity and the challenges life throws at us. Strength as resistance in the face of 'temptation'. Here, spirituality takes on the form of combat; and combat, in the form of renunciation, of *giving up*. The classic symbolism of demons and temptations are a way of illustrating this combat. To fall into temptation is to enter the cage, get trapped or addicted — to drugs, for example. To fight against the desire for power and riches, to fight against the desire for honour and prestige, to avoid eating and drinking too much, to avoid giving one's opinion on everything and, most important, to avoid judging all and sundry. This piece of advice is from another spiritual father: 'Sit in your cell, and if you are hungry, eat, if you are thirsty, drink; only do not speak evil of anyone, and you will be saved'.[4] In general, to not fall into excessiveness is evidence that, to live — even well — one doesn't need much. Indeed, the human situation is more a condition of scarceness than abundance — this, despite appearances created by our consumerist society. Hobbes says that it is from here — scarcity, together with the fact that we generally all want the same thing — that conflict arises. But what if we all got by with but a little? Contemporary civilisation has dedicated itself to paths diametrically opposed to this, dedicated as it is to consuming more and more, reaching further and further without stopping, and going ever faster. Even with all that, a little is enough. Ambition takes on many shapes and is a source of conflict and unrest. *Little is enough*. But also, (absolutely) necessary.

Finally, strength is resistance in the face of sadness. And so, what feeds strength? Where does it get its strength, its fortitude, from? All resistance lives in hope. The opposite of hope is not desperation, but rather a lack of hope in the sense of the weight

4. Anon. *The Saying of The Desert Fathers*, (tr. B. Ward), 1975

of which Kierkegaard speaks, or the bitterness and meaningless sadness (*acedia*) according to the scholars; or a tiredness that comes from considering everything to be in vain, that nothing is worth anything. Here, Marcel's phrase is both adequate and beautiful: 'Hope is perhaps the material from which our spirit is made'.

DEFINITIVE DEFEAT?

We have already said that resistance does not abandon but perseveres. It knows, however, that at times one must '*give way*'. In the end, tiredness cannot be resisted — one must sleep — and the vigil, which is resistance, is not defeated through this: after the pause, the watch continues. There are also moments of great impotence: the lighthouse watchman is unable to stop the shipwrecks in the midst of the terrible storm, and all that is left for him to do is to not abandon his watch, to remain attentive and hope for the best. Resistance is not resignation.

Human resistance knows neither victory, nor definitive defeat. By the same notion, therein lies something very special, or very strange, glimpsed even in the very worst scenarios, like that of the myth of Sisyphus who was, without doubt, a resister. It is precisely that which Camus very astutely highlights in his interpretation of the myth when he focusses on the moment in which, having pushed it to the top of the mountain, the rock starts to roll downwards once more with Sisyphus following it on foot:

'I see that man going back down with a heavy yet measured step toward the torment of which he will never know the end. That hour like a breathing-space which returns as surely as his suffering, that is the hour of consciousness. At each of those moments when he leaves the heights and gradually sinks toward the lairs of the gods, he is superior to his fate. He is stronger than his rock.'[5]

5. Albert Camus. *The Myth of Sisyphus and Other Essays* (tr. J. O'Brien), Vintage, 1991

The flash of awareness is at the same time condemned and recharged, though, and is a way of controlling the situation. Leaving the Sisyphus myth aside, that definitive victory does not exist simply means that there is no way of overcoming our own condition. Rendition might be reached when struggles are limited, when no energy remains to continue the resistance; one gives in due to faintness or desperation; one might pass on the baton: bear witness to this; some victories are achievable, though they are always provisional. They don't mean avoiding the next day's vigil and one's memory (which should never be lost). Defeat is, first and foremost, the persistence of the abyss of pain and, secondly, personal death. The first represents continuous defeat appeased only by moments of charity. The second seals the mystery of our condition. In the last departure, what are worst are the long, drawn-out agonies. Eyes of resignation, of impotency and acceptance. The agony is worse than the end. As such, despite the powerful feeling connecting us to life, there is also the desire to die, first bitterly and, having capitulated, more explicitly. How the gaze changes! It goes out, but a strangle gleam emerges from the fading light. A gleam that emerges from defeat: if its intensity were measured by its significance, this would be a lot more intense than the gleams of those juvenile moments in which the battle is hardly perceived. To live is not so much to live, but rather to be aware of it. The end of the finite is in no way the infinite, but the most finite of the finite; there, where finitude is most firmly expressed. After clarity of and about existence, nothing of it is perverse: neither the effort to stay alive, nor the act of giving in to sleep (at times induced). They are conditions of the capitulation, almost always both acceptable, sensible. The more familiar the last interval, the better. Again, *in extremis*, it is the salvation of proximity. The obligatory farewell is the prologue to a reunion with God, or to a chance meeting with eternal nothingness.

In any case, resistance would not have been in vain. Life as a form of resistance hopes not for immediate victory. It is not an 'optimistic' — among other things — resistance because, as García Lorca once said, optimism belongs to one-dimensional souls. Resistance, in no way superficial or banal, will never completely abandon joy, linked to the sense of that which is more essential and which provides meaning, linked to that which now provides the strength to hold on. The truly wise are not those who, with their own capacity for intellectual penetration, discover the order of the world through historical power; the real wise people are those who see that human excellence lies in this experience that is as profound as it is ambiguous: we have the privilege of realising this mystery (of the manifestation) of the world and our own selves, but see here that, at the same time, we grasp our finitude along with all of the sieges of evil. The wise response to this privilege consists of not giving in. Of not giving in to optimism. I agree with Marcel that: 'a spirit to which all anxiety is alien, is a perverted one.'[6] But neither should one give in to despondency, discouragement and weak-spiritedness.

Resistance is not irrational. Everything depends on this strange privilege we have through our relationship with the 'truth' (if we understand *truth* as a dialogue with all of existence). Neither optimism, nor despondency. The strength of resistance is neither tough nor apathetic; at its core it is sweet, even placid (adjectives that define the ways of the wise). It is therefore paradoxical that the tense, vigilant spirit is expressed through a relaxed face. The spirit tense from resisting is light and slight, showing little self-pride. Self-satisfaction has given way to dialogue: to interior dialogue (something that is, in fact, dialogue with the alterity found in the self) and to dialogue and communion with others. Narcissus' frustration is related to the impossibility of the unit, while the resister's fortune comes from the primacy of the *union* (dialogue is a type of union). The not being one with oneself and, what's more, not being one in terms of dialogue

6. Gabriel Marcel, *L'homme problématique* [*Problematic Man*], (tr. translator's own)

with others is more primordial than any unity.

Nothing of unity, though the possibility of *coming together*. To speak of depth is almost always directly or indirectly to speak of our depth and of the secret that lies within, though our ways and means of sounding out these depths are extremely limited. To descend is very difficult: no ladder exists. We soon find ourselves without rope, seemingly losing consciousness and sight. I refer not to asphyxia, as a descent down into a wine barrel might suggest: it is no lethal gas stemming from fermentation that impedes our way or intimidates us. It is simply that descending is difficult. But setting off is the beginning of coming together and of interior dialogue.

The path towards oneself lies next to the transformation of the day to day. Once again, care of the self is no escape, but the contrary: it is the *transformation of the day to day*. No ivory towers, no pretensions far from normal life. Rather than purity, creation requires silence. The philosopher should not, therefore, distance themself from the world, from life. Another thing is that the philosopher changes them through their point of view. The point of view coming from the care of the self is not 'merely' contemplative, it is also transformative. They are ideologies, those that send life to sleep or bury it. Care of the self is the door to its transfiguration. All things, the world, will be glimpsed in their mystery. It is a revelation that all constituted powers negate due to its strange ability to non-violently rock their very foundations.

VII. NOT GIVING IN TO THE DOGMATISM OF ACTUALITY

The current way of not counting is, paradoxically, being counted through statistics. Public opinion — which instead of being the manifestation of collective thought is, inversely, a manipulated object, consumers' (induced) inclinations, but most importantly the act of finding yourself thrust into that which the era sets out as a seemingly voluntarily accepted destination, are all signs of the success of dogmatism. All that dominates and can be assumed to be true, simply because it 'is', is dogmatic. The sugar-coated scepticism propounded by cut-price intellectuals is painful to watch as they belittle ancient gods and old beliefs while fanning the flames of new dogmas.

What is the most adequate way of resisting actuality? According to Jünger, might it be the notion of the forest rebel? Or perhaps — according to Deleuze[1] — the one who creates? Is there one reactionary resistance and another revolutionary one? Or perhaps, so as to see it a little clearer, is it worth simply avoiding the use, at least at the beginning, of this overused political dichotomy? Real resistance to actuality consists of *not giving in* to dogmatism. Nothing more, nothing less. At times it will take place under spotlights in the public eye; at others, it will be discreet and silent, knowing how to discern when one or the other is necessary. Though either way, it's no good complaining about either the lack of megaphones or headlines of repercussions. As Nietzsche says: 'When a human being resists his whole age and stops it at the gate to demand an accounting, this must have influence.'[2]

1. The formula repeated in various places is this: 'To think, to create, to resist'. And then emphasis: 'To create is not to communicate, but rather to resist'. Precisely due to the fact that the idea of communication inundates all (philosophy included): 'We lack not communication, but rather the opposite, we have too much; we lack creation. *We lack resistance to the present.*'
Gilles Deleuze, Qu'est-ce que la philosophie? [*What is Philosophy?*], (tr. translator's own)
2. Friedrich Nietzsche, *The Gay Science*, (tr. W. Kaufman), Vintage Books, 1974

Our age makes out as if the solution to the enigma of human life has been found and is no longer a secret: there is what there is, and we now know it all thanks to science. As Jan Patočka shows us, to not give in doesn't mean confessing the absurd or believing one to be in the perfect place (and knowing everything). Rather the contrary: it means accepting exposure to inhospitableness and problematicity. We have already said that nihilism, like the god Janus, has two faces: the empty one, and the full one. Two faces that, in our current age, we must know how to uncover, as only this way can we resist effectively. Though providing nourishment for both faces, the allies of the full face are more often than not the know-it-alls — sporting new masks —, the predomination of screens around the world, and technical-scientist (*not* scientific) ideology. The empty face is ally to 'selfish power', the modern-day politics serving actuality that aims, and is able, to absolve itself from commitments and responsibility (nobody's there on the other end of the line).

THE THREAT FROM (THE EVER PRESENT) KNOW-IT-ALLS

We are being overwhelmed by know-it-alls, a secular danger that can currently be found everywhere along with all sorts of social, pseudo-academic and media-based paraphernalia elevating it tenfold. Montaigne referred to it when he spoke of the: 'vain, frivolous subtleties through which men occasionally glimpse success.'[3] He recuperates the Socratic subject of well-versed ignorance:

Abecedarian ignorance that precedes knowledge, and a doctoral ignorance that comes after it: an ignorance that knowledge creates and begets, at the same time that it despatches and destroys the first.

3. Michel de Montaigne, *Essais* [*Essays*], (tr. translator's own)

Wise ignorance consists of realising that we know nothing of that which is most important. According to Montaigne, the worst and most pernicious is the middle part, made up of those who believe they have moved beyond primary ignorance and yet have not reached the second; they are both haughty and, without realising it, dogmatic people. As such, he writes:

'The simple peasants are good people, and so are the philosophers, or whatever the present age calls them, men of strong and clear reason, and whose souls are enriched with an ample instruction of profitable sciences. The mongrels who have disdained the first form of the ignorance of letters, and have not been able to attain the other (sitting betwixt two stools, as I and a great many more of us do), are dangerous, foolish and importunate; these are they that trouble the world. And therefore, it is that I, for my own part, retreat as much as I can towards the first and natural station, whence I so vainly attempted to advance.'

The same subject is also taken up by Pascal, in terms that require citation and so are shared here in full:

'The world is a good judge of things, for it is in natural ignorance, which is man's true state. The sciences have two extremes which meet. The first is the pure natural ignorance in which all men find themselves at birth. The other extreme is that reached by great intellects who, having run through all that men can know, find they know nothing, and come back again to that same ignorance from which they set out; but this is a learned ignorance which is conscious of itself. Those between the two, who have departed from natural ignorance and not been able to reach the other, have some smattering of this vain knowledge and pretend to be wise. These trouble the world and are bad judges of everything.'[4]

In effect, the know-it-alls, or *semi*-experts, supposed specialists in all manner of things, disrupt the world, speaking too

4. Blaise Pascal, *Pensées,* (tr. W.F. Trotter), CCEL, 2010

much when they should keep quiet. They are all answers and leave almost no room for the questions to which they have no answers. The amount of rubbish spouted *per capita* these days on the radio and television programmes, conferences and symposiums, has never been witnessed in the same proportion in any village café bar among simple folk playing cards on Sunday afternoons. And at least any nonsense reeled off in the bar is recognised as such.

The success of the semi-experts shows that the world fills too easily with meaning. And here we see that effort, so as not to give in to the void and nonsense, has to now be maintained in order to not give in to all rapid (and, as such, dogmatic) meanings. It is resistance before the empire of the void, but also before the collapse of acritical meaning. With this can be defined a condition that is these days radically different from that mentioned: it defines the human being very well and requires just as much tenacity not to give in to nothingness as not to give in to the presumed possessions of meaning.

Interesting is today one of the most readily used adjectives in strategies involving the possessed meaning, and a key word for know-it-alls. The society of the advertisement seeks out the most insistent and untiring way to affect undifferentiated members of the consuming masses and the response to this is expected to be: 'This is interesting'. And everything stops here, as anyone saying this really has nowhere else to go. 'Scientific' programmes related to the human being start with the phrase: 'We now know that...', as if the enigma of all enigmas (what are we?) has now been decoded, while it continues to be as enigmatic as ever. In the end, the only thing it does is to provoke another 'interesting', as ephemeral as it is superficial, and that will soon be displaced by another, newer one.

We have opted to talk about the *actual* rather than the *present* because the present, if not reduced and betrayed, has a depth that makes it *unrepresentable*. This is because it is linked to *giving*, and also because we hope to be able to explore it as one of the three conjoined axes of metaphysics after the end of metaphysics itself. Yet it is impossible to ignore the philosophical richness of the words *act* and *actuality*, both of which were highly relevant in Aristotle's works.[5] There is an Aristotelian philosophical construct that tries to avoid the problem of nothingness while accounting for movement; it is composed of two complimentary concepts: *dynamis* and *energeia*, translated — or, according to Heidegger, betrayed — into Latin as *potentia* and *actualitas*. Aristotle's intention is to substitute 'that which is in no way anything' for deprivation. The word *energeia* contains both the idea of activity and the realisation of potential. The problem with finally translating it into the word *actuality* is that this word suggests the result of an activity and not the activity itself. The thing is that these words and phrases have come to us because a number of centuries ago scholastic philosophy explained that all moveable beings were composed of act and potency. If that which is, is, then why is there movement? It was said, therefore, that it was because that which was there in potency is converted into act. The blooming flowers on a tree in spring are neither the manifestation nor the appearance of anything that was in no way nothing (nothing can come from nothing), nor the appearance of that which was hidden, but rather of something that was, but in a different form: in potency. The scholars were concerned not to exaggerate the radicalness of movement: it wasn't about understanding that everything came forth from a fountain bubbling away without drying up, but rather understanding that all things move towards their own perfectibility. Act is perfection. Movement

5. Especially Aristotle's *The Physics*

is actual in relation to one aspect and potency in relation to the other aspect. Reality is potency and act. A child is already actual in terms of many determinations or perfections, but with an actuality that is in part potency; as such, through movement it will be, in part, 'different' and will remain, in part, 'the same'. Potency is aptitude or order, determinability.

In this way of explaining things, potency (*dynamis*) is subordinate to the actual (*energeia*) and Heidegger is probably right when he warns that the dominance of actuality leads to incomprehension both in terms of *dynamis* and *energeia*. The empire of actuality, in fact, marginalises movement and, with movement, time. Thus, the dominance of actuality is the disappearance of time. Everything is actual. We turn everything into subject predicates and destroy our attention to movement. We say that A is B, when what should be recognised is the movement from A to B, from one thing to another. In this last part there is a difference: 'one thing' and 'another thing'. In other words, movement and time. Through the balancing out of things or the suppression of difference, however, everything can be treated as objective and controllable. Actuality is everything, it monopolises all. Even possibility. There are things we don't know yet or that we are still unable to produce. But this is already determined within the very same actuality. And in this way, being has ceased to refer to differences, instead only referring to expansion.

When today we say *actuality*, we are in fact serving its dominance, though we have made an important variation. *Actuality* is now the *anticipation of the* (ever immediate) *future*. To be aware of actuality is to know that which has already arrived, as if the future were coming towards us. The future is the potency, while the now is the progressive realisation of this potency. And here we are, turned into servants — not to mention slaves — to the actualisation of the future.

The recently mentioned rhetoric of the semi-experts combines well with the regime of connected information and constant screens, a regime without day or night and in constant flux. One might say: 'a day without night', but a day in which the light is unchanging as it is no lighter in the morning or dimmer in the evening. This strange day is called 'actuality'. Let us emphasise this: more than it being about maturing and a process leading to a greater perfection, it is about *anticipation*. As such, the patience and temporariness belonging to maturity do not wed themselves to actuality. Actuality as anticipation sooner promotes expectation and urgency so as not to lose that which in each moment is actual. The fact that *screen*, *world*, and *current* are identified with each other comes from this common trait: they are spilling over. It is now no longer only the cultural industry (denounced by those from the Frankfurt School) that organises and subtly fills up free time (or, the void), but everything.

Resistance to the empire of actuality comes from memory and imagination. One and the other resist the operation of actuality as it abandons the past, erases it, before making the status quo — now bubbling into our lives from the future — out to be the be-all and end-all. That memory and imagination are going through their worst moments only serves to certify the efficiency of its dominance. And who are we without memory? The simple folk 'knew', too, that there is something of worth in the memory of a life. Memory is not a memory of the past, but the ampliation and enrichment of the present. It is only through memory that time now passed is not finished and that the present (that which 'is present' to us) is not reduced to — and betrayed by — actuality. Resistance inevitably starts when looking back. Science, like political rhetoric, is always looking forward. But the gesture most closely associated with thought is that which turns and looks backwards. And it is then that things start to rumble and the absurd begins to threaten. The main problem is looking back. And while not as much of a problem, today looking sideways is starting to become problematic. Whereas to be watchful of actuality is evasion, abstraction and flight. And here we have the connection to technoscience. While one of the main imperatives in which thought is seen to be confronted is that nothing that has happened can be annulled, technoscientific logic works in another way, tending towards the direction of omnipotence and a continuing opening of possibilities.

Actuality has no thickness: it is flat. Full, but flat. And short. Full of data, of information; not of worldly information but rather of information about the world. The information is not a means, but the configuration of the world. Because of this, information refers to yet more information. A 'world of information' is not a metaphor; it sucks on the material world — on the elements and bodies — and, worryingly, brings about new types of alienation. From Marx onwards we learned to denounce the alienation of workers perpetrated by the capitalist system, yet now a new form of alienation, more efficient than ever seems to be underway, and all of us are diving in without regret. The network fascinates and consumes and nothing or very little remains of anything intimate; everything is externalised, everything is put on show, and there is no return. This is the precise definition of alienation: that which goes out and never comes back. The withering of the spirit, of personality, of oneself. Adorno said that organised culture cuts access to the last possibility for men to experience themselves. This process has grown exponentially: now is the reign of actuality that, having emptied the world and replaced it, turns its attention to us so as to further remove any possibility of experience. This distancing has also been called 'objectivism' and 'representation'. We externalise ourselves by converting ourselves into data and images (that are also a form of data). The empire of actuality is the empire of images and the absence of imagination. The alienation of oneself, carried out with such fluidity, feeds into and yet at the same time hides an enormous frustration. The world of actuality traps and imposes itself as an apparently implacable destination, this in stark contrast to the ancient Moirai who didn't save humans from the weight of the decision.

To resist in the *non-actual* means to position yourself at the margins, to the flanks, and from there protect the difference. If 're-presentation' (and especially the thousand and one theories) dominates, then it is to maintain in the non-actual the link with that which cannot be represented (and that reveals itself as a trace or as responsibility). If the spectre of that which is foreseeable dominates, then it is not abandoning the unforeseeable (the difference) and even the impossible. The non-actual is neither the adhesion to facts, nor the anticipation of the optimum, but rather adhesion to the impossible that the past, though made impossible, protects. There are institutions such as universities that, instead of remaining in the non-actual, have given in and surrendered to actuality with willing servitude. Socrates is no less non-actual than Nietzsche.

Actuality is the emergence of the impersonal forces that dominate the world and control all they touch. Though we leave the study of political resistance aside, I note only that being taken from a position in the face of domination tends to be characterised by a series of elements: a *saying no* in the name of liberty and of *integrity* (the threat is that of disintegration); a clandestine combat voluntarily undertaken though there seems to be no other alternative (the situation demands resistance); and great importance placed on memory (a memorial to that which has already disappeared but that we wish to save, and the memory of the idealistic horizon of the non-actual community). The movements of political resistance, understood as such, are the best expression of the political essence: full of conscience, memory, hope and action.

No action programmes exist for the non-actual. There is, however, this: that no matter what it is, if authentic, it glows as a witness. In a book called *La Resistencia*, Ernesto Sábato confesses that his motto is the following: that one must resist, though it is not easy to find the most adequate way of embodying this expression. It has to have something to do — he says — with the act of maintaining hope as a candle might during the night of the world, while also — and necessarily — maintaining one's dedication to the weakest. Those who sacrifice themselves to care for unfortunates are without doubt those who best embody resistance. It seems significant that Sábato's spiritual testament brings together *night, resistance, hope* and *dedication,* and also that one of the conclusions he reaches is the following: 'We save ourselves through affection'. In other words, that which comes from the *heart.* The fatidic actuality, dominated by competitiveness and riven with violence, contrasts with the non-actuality of *heart, agape* or 'peaceful states' (to use an expression from Ricoeur).[6]

Though Nietzsche ridicules Socrates' ugliness — apparently Socrates was ugly — he fails to laugh at his capacity for resistance. How could he? Plutarch wrote that: 'Patience is more powerful than strength'. The imperious strength of actuality will never be able to destroy the resistance of the non-actual. And it's because of this that resistance is so concerning for the established power. Though the non-actual is marginal, it doesn't back down easily. On occasion, a young Socrates would stand, meditating, until sunrise. In his old age he didn't fear the dominant social power, facing up to it and staring it down just as he did with death.

That resistance is a reaction doesn't mean that it's 'reactionary'. Resistance is reaction in the face of dominating and disintegrating forces. And because of this, a free, creative space opens up. To create is related to the fact that something new appears, but also with the fact that this process means a personal, infinite and contagious (in other words, affecting others) transformation. Let actuality seem not a burden, let its homogeneity not offend us, and let its dogmatism be revised and criticised. Either we resist or the community of free men and women will have no

6. These themes, along with that which Adorno calls the 'perspective of redemption' (and that is another name for the *inactual*), deserve their own, separate consideration.

future; no meaning, no memory. Actuality promotes and demands fascination. Humility is also an answer, and in no way in vain is humility alien to fascination; it is not dazzled, remaining on its pilgrimage, guided by a place under the heavens where the hours and halls, in no way pharaonic, will finally bear their fruit.

While actuality conceals the abyss of this world and pathologizes existence (if one night someone suffers from fear or panic, what is recommended is that they look for some adequate therapy for their psychological disorder), resistance looks the abyss in the eyes. And thanks to this, one can recuperate words and offer out their hand. Resistance has multiple, intertwining, open battlefronts: the state of numb, inert things; history as totality; injustice and destruction; stupidity. Actuality includes all of these, concealing or empowering them, depending on the case.

There is life beyond actuality. Or better said: life only exists beyond actuality. Life, liberty and thought are given laterally. Freedom consists of leaving the statistics to one side and heading out to the margins so as to create, to resist. The marginal condition represents prime numbers in the sense that they can't be split. And precisely because splitting them is not possible, they come together and multiply.

Moment

Cities in ruins, dust and fire, murky waters and smells, grey sky and parched land... Often these are the elements used to produce images of devastation, disasters at the end of the world, or the consequences of tomorrow. At times the figure of a survivor wanders perplexed in the midst of this chaos, their eyes wide, their gaze lost. A host of literary and cinematographic stories have employed this fictitious scene, sustained in good part by the imaginary link to nuclear war.

But now a different image. Just a few years ago a marginal controversy simmered along regarding the construction of a powerful and 'highly advanced' particle accelerator. Obviously, the thing that interests us here is not so much scientific accuracy, but the work of the imagination. According to a current theory, one of the 'frontal collisions' between these subatomic particles accelerated to astronomical speeds might produce a small black hole. Now, this is highly improbable, and even more improbable that this mini black hole might somehow grow and consume everything around it. This black hole would have an extremely high surface-mass ratio leading it to 'sweat' a lot — *sweat* here meaning the emission of radiation. It would sweat so much that the poor thing would disappear almost instantaneously. But were one of these improbable mini black holes strong enough not to collapse despite the loss of energy and last just long enough to swallow itself and start to grow, then the end would be sealed: the mini black hole would swallow the entirety of our beloved planet in a heartbeat. An absolutely singular end: no waste, clean, aseptic and, above all, quick and painless. The black hole would become the most effective and perfect global euthanasia. Like a gulp of water, a swig of earth: the world swallows itself and we vanish without even realising it.

VIII. THE OCEAN OR THE DESERT?

The desert and ocean are the two great irreconcilable metaphors of the human condition. What combines well with the intention of guiding these pages is the metaphor of the desert (the *surface* of the ocean is desert). Shelter only makes sense in the desert, not in the ocean. There is no immersion in the desert. The stretched out human profile is like a hook that unites both earth and the heavens; a vertical line upon the vast extension of the earth and under a sky that is, at the same time, relentless and protective. No, the desert is no ocean. There, the wanderer carves out their route by following the course of the sun as it moves from east to west. The elements, with their immensity and toughness, accompany, however, the path of the mortal. To lose oneself in the desert is not to dissolve: it is death.

But we are with others. In other words, it is slap bang in the middle of the desert plain where the face of the other appears when and where it requires a warm welcome. My willingness, expressed through this gesture towards the other, is willingness in the desert; it is a willingness precisely *due* to the desert. The planet is round, but the earth is flat like a plane, and upon this boardwalk we wander, following the itinerary of our lives, until the very end, until we run out of strength. It is an end not marked by a wall. Rather, it is the earth that reclaims us, and the little strength that still keeps you upright gives way; not a wall, but the gravity of the horizon.

On the plane (a plain, no less), we mortals wander until the despondency of predicted ends, but with one's own inner drive and the encouragement from those close to us. On the plane (a plain, no less), we mortals wander, enveloped by the cold above and the hardness of the ground below. On the plane (a plain, no less), they ask for shelter and beg for words. On the plane (a plain, no less), there is no way of rising up above the roofs of the houses towards the eternal heavens, nor can one bury oneself in the rigid strata of the earth. This situation determines both gesture and thought. You can dream, yes, and escape, and feel yourself rising up like children's kites or hot air balloons. But afterwards, you must come back down to the plain. It's better not to weigh yourself down, but neither should you relinquish your whole ballast, as — along with the ballast — you might leave your spirit behind.

The desert illustrates the precariousness of the human condition. It is no coincidence that the words *prayer* and *precarious* share the same root. Precariousness gives meaning to shelter. There is no shelter in the ocean; only immersion and dissolution. In the desert, there is welcoming and death. There are no words in the ocean or, if there are, they belong to the discourse of totality: capital letters, rounded words, and circular discourse. In the desert, the word is a tent. The universal (divine?) *Logos* is of the ocean, and prayer is of the desert. And a long line of thought has brought the universal and divine *Verb*, *Logos*, and *Reason* together. The essence of human language has nothing to do with this. And, luckily, it seems that some clairvoyant theologian has stated that not even the word God has anything to do with it. Religion is a desert (sandy, urban, navigational, etc.) experience, not an oceanic one. Freud was right when he said that, rather than a 'feeling of the ocean', the origin of religiousness is the experience of helplessness. He would have been able to argue that it is a primarily infantile experience (though he himself recognised that it was not just infantile), just as this experience is easily converted into a thesis of illusion.

Let's remember how these things went. In his 1927 book, *Die Zukunft einer Illusion* (*The Future of an Illusion*), Freud published a text that was to analyse the psychological significance of religious ideas, his 'psychiatric genesis'. In this, he maintains that: 'Religions are illusions, realisations of the most ancient, intense and urgent desires of humanity.'[1] And that: 'God was

1. Sigmund Freud, *The Future of an Illusion*, (tr. J. Strachey), WWN&C, 1961

the exalted father, and the longing for the father was the root of the need for religion.'[2] This same idea is repeated in Freud's 1930 work, *Das Unbehagen in der Kultur* (*The Uneasiness in Civilisation*): 'The derivation of religious needs from the infant's helplessness.'[3] It therefore deals with an early sense of angst when faced with one's destiny, which then reappears in adulthood. So, let us use this thesis by which he puts into context that which is of most interest to us, and which is the focus of a discussion that, at the very beginning of *Das Unbehagen in der Kultur*, that Freud (referring to Romain Rolland) has with a friend of his. The background to this discussion is this: Freud sends Rolland a copy of *Die Zukunft einer Illusion* and, later, Rolland writes Freud a letter telling him he doesn't understand why, in his book, Freud made no mention of the underlying source of religion which, according to Rolland, is a sensation of eternity, the feeling of which has no limits or barriers and is 'oceanic' in its manner.[4] Rolland agrees with Freud that religion is an illusion, but laments that Freud: 'had not properly appreciated the true source of religious sentiments'. He suggests that he, like most human beings, would have shared this oceanic feeling, a feeling thanks to which: 'One may ... rightly call oneself religious on the ground of this oceanic feeling alone, even if one rejects every belief and every illusion.'

Freud confesses that what his friend says places him in an awkward situation as: 'I cannot discover this 'oceanic' feeling in myself.' Despite this, he is willing to see what this feeling might contain and, in fact, while possessing it, he is capable of describing it even better than his friend. Freud writes: 'That is to say, it is a feeling of an indissoluble bond, of being one with the external world as a whole.' He adds that, according to him, rather than it being a feeling, it's a form of intellectual penetration accompanied by, oh yes, emotional undertones. In attempting a

2. *Ibid.*
3. Sigmund Freud, *Civilisation and its discontents*, (tr. J. Strachey), WWN&C, 2010
4. *Ibid.*

psychoanalytical (in other words, genetic) explication for the oceanic feeling, Freud refers to the first few months of life when the ego is the same as the id. At the very beginning, the ego is everything but, slowly but surely, differences emerge between the two. Experience, and especially experience of pain, starts to separate the pleasurable ego from a problematic exterior. As such, while humans would feel as if the mother's breast formed part of the same being, later, when having to cry for it, the difference would start to appear. It's not too difficult to see the relationship that might be established between the oceanic feeling and the lack of difference in which the infant might find itself, without an inside and an out. Once described in this way, Freud argues that, in terms of religiousness, this feeling is *secondary* to that which is truly important:

'I cannot think of any need in childhood as strong as the need for a father's protection. Thus, the part played by the oceanic feeling, which might seek something like the restoration of limitless narcissism, is ousted from a place in the foreground.'[5]

Having already discussed it above, I move away from this suggestive addendum on narcissism. While not being the most primordial, Freud admits that the oceanic feeling has a religious dimension because it presents a kind of *consolation*; its conceptual contents (being one with everything) would reduce or even annul the conflict and the non-agreement between the ego and the exterior world. That's to say that in adults, while the sought-after union with everything would fade away — though this doesn't happen with Freud or, and I say this with all modesty, with me — the angst produced through helplessness and destiny would increase. Within this type of generic thought, one might discover different, variously named, 'techniques' by which one might leave behind one's ego and achieve access to

5. *Ibid.*

the Divine Whole.

It was an interview with Pierre Hadot,[6] a French historian of ancient philosophy, that led us to pick up this old polemic surrounding the 'oceanic feeling'. When looking back to his philosophical awakening, Hadot explains that as a young man he:

'experienced a strange feeling of surprise and wonder of being. But at the same time I had the feeling of being submerged in the world, of forming part of this world that extended from the tiniest organic wisps up to the stars. I was intensely aware of this world. Later, I realised that this increased consciousness from my immersion in the world, this sense of belonging to All, was that which Romain Rolland had called the 'oceanic feeling'. I believe I have been a philosopher from that moment onwards, if one can, through philosophy, understand this consciousness of existence, of being-in-the-world.'[7]

To better mark the boundaries of what this feeling involves, he adds that it is necessary to distinguish it from a simple admiration inverse Nature; the oceanic feeling means seeing oneself as truly a wave within a limitless ocean, understanding oneself as part of a mysterious, infinite reality. He stresses that the impression of *immersion* is very important, the space between the I and the Other that, rather than being a foreign body, actually forms a part. Importantly, Hadot, who was very well versed in ancient thought, recognises that this is a feeling that is quite alien to Christian thought, and he doubts whether the Greeks, having spoken little of this *immersion*, would have fully developed this idea. They would have had the partial idea, true, and it is for precisely this reason that, within the discussion that Hadot had with Foucault about the Greeks' interpretation of care of the self, one of Hadot's criticisms was that Foucault hadn't placed

6. Pierre Hadot, *La philosophie comme manière de vivre* [*Philosophy as a Way of Life*], Albin Michel, 2001.
7. *Ibid.* (tr. translator's own)

enough attention on the importance of belonging to a cosmic Whole, and the combined human community.[8] Of course Hadot, here agreeing with Freud, is aware of the comforting role played by this oceanic feeling: as it's both an overcoming of the 'partial self', and a way of learning to die. We can see, therefore, that in both the Freud-Rolland argument and Hadot's autobiographical description, the role attributed to the oceanic feeling is the same.[9]

I consider Freud to have also been splitting hairs when he observed that it was not just a simple feeling, but that it was made up of both emotional and intellectual elements. It is not difficult to identify cases in which almost all of the emphasis is placed on conceptual work; on work that produces exactly the 'same' result as the oceanic feeling. I am reminded of the magnificent beginning to Franz Rosenzweig's 1921 work, *Die Philosophie des Erlösung* (*The Star of Redemption*), a description of the conceptual process that idealistic philosophy follows so as to dissolve the entirety of the supposed singularity in a sole generic concept corresponding to a single reality. This is what he says: humans know they are mortal, and so have to overcome fear of death; a fear that, despite desires they cannot be freed of, found as it is in the very essence of the human condition, in our earthly situation and that, as such, *has to* be tolerated. It is against this backdrop that he makes philosophical 'salvation' present:

'Philosophy tricks [the mortal] through this *has to* by bringing together that which is earthly with the smoky blue thought of the Whole. This is because, of course, a Whole does not die, just as nothing dies in the Whole. [...] Once trapped in this foggy cocoon, death is swallowed up, if not by eternal victory, but then by the one, universal night of nothingness.'[10]

8. *Ibid.* (tr. translator's own)

9. Regarding the oceanic feeling, it is worth Reading Michel Hulin's book, which Hadot also refers to: Michel Hulin, *La mystique sauvage*, PUF, 1993.

10. Franz Rosenzweig, *Die Philosophie des Erlösung* [*The Star of Redemption*], tr. translator's own).

See here the role of Totality: to suck away death and, through this, the fear of death. To do this, however, it needs to first dissolve any singularity into the Whole, and the conceptual function of philosophy is just this: to disconnect oneself from any kind of singular, converting it into merely a part of the Whole. Yet — adds Rosenzweig, most incisively — despite philosophy and its integratory fog's praiseworthy consolatory intention, mortal angst remains that, without alleviation, continues upon the battlefield of the world: 'The angst of the man who trembles before this needle's thrusts always rigorously denies the white, compassionate lie of philosophy'. In the guises of History, Nature, or Absolute Spirit, the philosophies of Totality have tried towards a kind of integration-dissolution of the singulars into the Whole, but an experience of the self — consciousness of one's own finitude along with the finitude of the you — resists, time and again, in the face of any kind of dissolution, and the remedy never really has an effect.

Though there are always attempts to resuscitate the Totality, the truth is that if one is just a little rigorous, it is far from easy. We are living, as has already been stated, in the wake of a nihilistic shock, and Nietzsche himself directly and very efficiently attacked the category of the Unit endowed with meaning (with consolation included). And, within the field of experience, the one field that truly counts, the oceanic feeling is scarcer than might be imagined. Often without even realising, contemporary humans are accompanied by a biblical inheritance to which is added the effects of the nihilistic storm. It is the case that, when all is said and done, today's experience is more about existing in the open. As Camus says, we may revolt (resist) and still be capable of obtaining a meaning, but long before anything else the situation is far from perfect. The existentialist background strongly coincides — without of course identifying itself as doing so — with the typical agnostic arguments that, as the agnostic Harold Bloom reminds us, are the following: 'First, the estrangement, even the alienation of God, who has abandoned this cosmos, and second, the location of a residuum of divinity in the Gnostic's own inmost self.'[11]

A central, or perhaps ambivalent, position is, in this case, no concession. It is that which, despite distractions and proposals of diverse types, responds with most affinity to our age-old experience; we realise that we form part of the world, in which we are somehow integrated; but that at the same time we don't quite belong in this reality, that it somehow separates us from all that we call the *world* and that we seem to have before us. Not so much at sea, like a breaking wave, human beings are on the rocks, next to the wharf, *before* the immensity. An immensity that, as Pascal says, both calms and terrifies us.

Here, we can ask ourselves: what relationship is there between the ocean of everything and the nihilism of nothingness? As we have already insinuated above, we believe that it is through this that we can reach a most revelatory interpretation of the nihilistic experience, the emphasis of which can be found in the meaning, or the absurd. The decisive difference is no longer between the being and nothingness, but rather between the meaning and the absurd. Paradoxically, through this displacement, nothingness and being come so close together as to almost touch. To illustrate this, the use of Blanchot's and Levinas' concept of *il y a* (there is) is most adequate.

What is the *there is*? Well, undifferentiated reality; darkness and background noise; childhood fear of the dark and the impossibility of making out anyone's voice. The background hum of being and nothingness coincide. In order to explain this experience, one can turn once more to Antoine Roquentin, the protagonist of Sartre's *Nausea*: 'Does the gooeyness of existence not amalgamate into an undifferentiable *there is*?' That said, so as not to abuse this idea more than is necessary, we will mention another, less well-known, character from the film *Il*

11. Harold Bloom, *Omens of Millennium*, Riverhead, 1996.

Deserto Rosso, by Michelangelo Antonioni, played by Monica Vitti. The film is set in a heavily industrialised area in the Po Delta, close to Ravenna. The factories, the machines, gears and gases produce, from the very beginning, a disquieting sensation related to the act of depersonalisation. Giuliana is the wife of an engineer, the director of one of these factories. As you might guess, Giuliana doesn't work, and her status allows her a daily life most distinct from that of the workers and her husband. In fact, it is as if she didn't have a daily life. And precisely because she is not integrated into this life, Giuliana has a different perspective of this technological world, leading her to launch into research on the meaning of life and its things. In one of the first scenes, a wandering Giuliana comes across some striking workers. She is clearly far removed from the daily problems these workers have; she is in another 'orbit' from where nothing in this homogeneous, monochrome world seems to have any meaning. Giuliana experiences an existential angst that her husband attributes to a recent car crash and that, as such, he does not understand. She needs meaning and communication and is suffocated by the situation. Likewise, she finds day-to-day language meaningless: she needs other words, other registers, other tones of speech. Here we have the sensation of being imprisoned and of angst and the necessity of finding a way out: a way out of the insomnia of an undifferentiated reality rolling on uninterrupted. The undifferentiated *there is* and the greyness of the world as perceived by Giuliana is as absurd as nothingness.

IX. THE ESSENCE OF LANGUAGE AS SHELTER

GOING FORWARD

The first word is of petition, and the second, shelter. The question is the daughter of petition. After *rogare* — the act of petitioning, of imploring, of requesting — we in turn interrogate ourselves. Philosophy is simply self-questioning: we ask *ourselves*. Weeping and shouting: 'A cry of distress cannot be greater than that of one human being', wrote Wittgenstein.[1] Cry and petition, and petition and interrogation are expressions of the first part of the movement of existence; later follow the different expressions of welcome.

To petition doesn't require saying anything. A request can be entirely mute. One speaks with one's eyes, and a gaze can petition, just as a look can both answer and welcome. As such, the *mother tongue* refers to the *mother word*, and the *mother word* is a reiteration because the word is maternal: it's a word of welcome. Before *infants* — those who are yet to talk — learn their mother tongue, the tongue has already received the child and has served as its home. And this language, before representing — according to Heidegger — the house of the being, is the house of the *human* being.

Déu vos guard! (*God bless you!*) is a traditional Catalan expression that, like so many others, is slowly disappearing. And it's not that it has anything to do with the general use of *Hola*, or the more informal, *Ei!* It has, in fact, been more widely replaced by, first mechanical and then electronic, doorbells. Before, during the day, front doors in Catalonia were not normally locked and, as one entered, one would shout: '*Déu vos guard!*' or '*Au Maria!*' But we are not here to discuss the social trends currently affecting language, but rather to reflect on the primordial meaning behind

1. Ludwig Wittgenstein, *Culture and Value*, (tr. P. Winch), Blackwell Publishers, 1998.

it. *Déu vos guard!* is, however, an expression that still has a lot in common with its primordial meaning; today it is an out of place expression that, under the guise of an automatic greeting, still contains a very petition-like intention.

In fact, this also closely coincides with something that Derrida said in his oration at his friend Levinas' funeral. From Levinas he learned — says Derrida — to say the word *adéu* (*Goodbye* or, literally, *Go to God*) in another way — as opposed to the automated nature of the habitual farewell, of course, but probably not very different from its first meaning. *Adéu* or *Déu vos guard!* mean the same thing: protection and shelter. They are literally salutations (of meeting and leaving) or, in other words, phrases that desire health (*salut*) and salvation for the other person. And it's for the same reason that we often say *Salut* (*Good health*), which has its equivalents in the Arabic *Salam* and Hebrew *Shalom*. Likewise, *Que et vagi bé* (*Fare thee well*) is an ancient greeting that manifests the desire that things in life and the general situation — rather than anything specific — go well for the person. In these times of God's absence, it is perhaps not surprising that the religious *adéu* is more regularly substituted by *cuida't* (*Take care*), though it would be even better to say *que et cuidin* (*Be cared for*). Is there anything better than this? Might it be that the care offered by others is the same as the care offered by God?

We can agree that sincerity is more valuable than accurate information. We value the word of a friend who speaks to us sincerely — despite perhaps being wrong — more than entirely objective information given to us impersonally. Parallel to this, lies, verbal violence and insults (the complete opposite of frank words) are all much more upsetting than errors (the opposite of the objective truth). Does this not show us that, when it comes to speech, affective and existential function is more 'essential' than the truth — understood as the link between the proposition and reality? And it's not that this last element doesn't count — it does, a lot — but it's just that, in the end, truth is upheld by sincerity, and this is the sap that circulates around the deepest roots of language.

ON THE TRAIL

Could the already mentioned affirmation that the essence of language is protection have anything to do with the 'linguistic turn' of contemporary philosophy? We know that this linguistic turn consists of giving philosophical priority to the transcendental question (in other words, a question about the conditions of possibility): 'How is language possible?' And we know, too, that this question has received two groups of answers: the first group, centred on Wittgenstein and Russell, determines a structured logic of language, and understands the most basic function of language as that of description. Language is primarily used to give sense to the world, announcing it and establishing within it what are things and facts. As such, what is important is the *proposition* (a linguistic unit that describes a fact) and its correspondence with reality (true or false). For example: 'The table is round' or 'It is raining'. In these kinds of statements, the propositional attitudes can be seen as being derived from, or constructed upon, the elemental proposition: '*I want* it to rain'. This propositional theory is linked to the noun theory: objects are named, and facts are described. As such, the first phase of the philosophy of language is characterised by research into the logical and semantic conditions of a perfect language: of a language, therefore, that correctly describes the states of things in the world.

But it is precisely this intention (that of the perfect language) that was set aside in the second group of responses to the previously mentioned question: 'How is language possible?', led by the very same Wittgenstein. Not, then, in *Tractatus*, but rather in his work, *Philosophical Investigations*. At that time, the assumption was not that logic would illuminate us on the structure of language and reality, but that ordinary language is richer than logic and that, as such, should have preference when dealt with in terms of philosophical research. The 'second' Wittgenstein believes that there is no unique 'essence' in general language, and that there is a great diversity of linguistic phenomena that can be grouped together depending on the type of traits they share with others. They are *language-games* and, in the same way that there is no single characteristic that defines different types of games, there is no single linguistic function to define language. Consequently, the theory of meaning would have to pay attention to the use of language as the language-game is the connection between a language and actions. The objective is not, therefore, to produce a classification of the different propositions according to their structure and meaning of the words, but instead to describe linguistic uses. In other words, semantics is replaced by pragmatics. The baton of this kind of thought was firmly grasped by Austin through the relatively eloquent title to his work: *How to Do Things with Words*. Through this, philosophical reflection on language came to form part — a particularly important one — of the reflection on action.

After this change of tack, is it still possible to ask our question about the essence of language? What more could be said apart from the fact that it deals with a type of action, and with a type of action within which lie distinguishable types of linguistically different actions: informative, communicative, evaluative, exclamative, imperative, etc.? Perhaps one of these registers is the primordial one? This, for example, is what Habermas has done in his *The Theory of Communicative Action* as he not only places it at the centre of his ethical and philosophical theory, but at the same time as being specifically human: through language, humans are offered their own emancipation as human beings. The communicative function of language, aiming primarily to *understand each other*, would be the primordial function of language, distinct from instrumental or strategic actions and, clearly, directly contrary to lies, control or violence.

Yet today a distinct direction — for obvious reasons — that carries a lot of weight is the concept of language as 'information': indeed, that this term has been transformed into an era-defining expression (The Age of Information) confirms this. The strength of seeing things this way comes from the confluence of two sources: on the one hand, that of the current dominance of information technology through the creation of global information networks; and on the other, that of the biological theories that define all organisms (humans included) as system-units capable of processing information. Within this general framework, the term *communication* tends to be interpreted as a transmission of information, and the information itself, as a confirmation of how things are. So that, when all is said and done, language continues to be interpreted primarily as a descriptive discourse and a processing and exchange of informative data. To this current concept of information is linked one of the traditional ways of reading the old description of a human being as an animal furnished with *logos*: a being with discursive capabilities that is able to give things names, explain the world, and exchange visions of said world. As such, despite the pragmatic inflexions of language through contributions as relevant as Habermas', the enunciative-informative register remains the dominant one.

This persistence, however, doesn't remove — on the contrary — the opportunity to ask once again: Is there a way of speaking (a radical or *arch*-gesture) that is deeper than the others and that, at least in part, the others are related to? A gesture that is different from that of information exchange and the discursive and enunciative gestures of the world. Could petition and protection be the two forms of this *arch-gesture*? Then, in the words *shelter* and *petition*, might we discover the path that leads us to the essence of speech (a path, however, that while not leading to a different place, it is rather already there at its destination; a path that leads not to any different region from that in which the path itself is sketched out and that, without being uselessly circular, provides meaning and a roof over our heads). And, as has already been stated, it is not a double response but rather the indication of the very same movement of existence: welcome follows petition (or imploring), and petition follows the welcome. This would not be — is not — a pious thesis in so far as it is a search coming from a pious perspective; it is philosophical: it strives to understand a little more or, simply, a little. Despite all this, it is true that this very same thesis is related to piety because it is directly related to caring for the other. *Shelter* or *welcome* refer specifically to that which would impressively emerge from the question: 'How are you?', if we were able to remove the inertial movement that so often guides it. It is in no way a banal question; despite the fact it is used vacuously so many times. The fact that in personal meetings one of the first expressions is: 'How are you?', is both fortunate and a revelation. The depth of the: 'How are you?' is the same as that of the: *'Déu vos guard!'* (Profound intentions that are equally lost within the folds of habit, indifference, and neglect).

To seek out the essence doesn't mean turning one's nose up at anything else, rather the contrary: it is perfectly apt to seek out the greatest depths by that which is already sustained by itself. Instead of discarding, therefore, it is better to attend to the resonance of the essence, that which can be heard in song, in the poetic world-creating, communicative and even the informative word.

SINGING TO WARD OFF FEAR

'Qui canta, el seu mal espanta' (*Those who sing, scare evil away*) is an old popular saying. 'Those who sing', affectionately say the

world, life, and themselves. Song expresses an essential knowledge of the situation; though not a precise understanding from an 'objective' point of view, it is a point of view that is relevant to the meaning derived from a particular connection with the world. It is this: the richness of the world is not to be found in argumentative or communicative constructs, but rather in the tonality and chordal variations that redirect the frequency of different things towards our internal synthesiser. This is the reason why the best poetry (if good, then it is also song) is that which is able to reconnect; it's poetry of those words through the tone of which the wonder of the synapse is renewed. It doesn't take much to see that many traces of song have been lost in the monotone language of information.

Poetry and song ask for and seek out the other and are neither the beginning nor the end of the conversation. An authentic dialogue is like a song with two voices. We say the world and ourselves, and to say is to think. Because of this, dialogue — thinking together — is much more than a simple exchange; it's contact and company that explains and celebrates the world while protecting us at the same time. A poem by a modest local poet, recited by an elderly woman with the strength of experience has no parallel. How is it that no intellectual excellence can get close to this? Well, because both poet and woman know how to connect with the sounds of objects, of situations, of the world. But also, most importantly, because a song can rise up high without lifting its feet up off the ground. The woman reciting the poem achieves this, in part, thanks to her experience of maternity and care. Her voice knits the blue of the heavens together with the sheltering home just as the mother sings to ward away her child's fear. Indeed, a maternal song is, in fact, a prayer, just as these beautiful verses by Giovanni Pascoli suggest:

Children pass: a murmur of tears;
a mother passes: a prayer passes.

[Passano bimbi: un balbettìo di pianto; |
passa una madre: passa una preghiera].[2]

Likewise, when a little older, the child will also sing to drive their own fear away. Song calms us when faced with darkness and shadows, while also protecting us from spiritual chill. In his novel *Disgrace*, writer Coetzee writes: '... the origins of speech lie in song, and the origins of song in the need to fill out with sound the overlarge and rather empty human soul.'[3] In terms of what we are trying to defend here, it is truly difficult to find a happier quote than this. That in spite of our love for Deleuze's perfect comment in *ritornello* about the song that the child, scared out of his wits, uses to calm and protect themself; a leap out of chaos towards the beginning of order, from being lost to being found, from being paralysed to taking their first steps.[4] The song with multiple voices is even better as the fabric of the song protects and shields still more. The song does not dissolve those who sing, but rather links them, brings them together, connects them with other things, with the world, with other people.

FROM INFORMING TO THE FORMING GESTURE

Contrary to poetic language and song, both of which remain close to the essence, the domain of information falls very far from the tree. Today we talk about 'being informed' in the sense of having both encyclopaedic knowledge about various things and in the sense of 'having news' about that which happens in the world. Information is like popular scientific discourse: it is a continuously growing summary of 'knowledge' and news, as if the world were a shelf of products and facts, each of them

2. From the poem 'Nevicata' by Giovanni Pascoli, Myricae, 2005. (tr. translator's own).
3. J. M. Coetzee, *Disgrace*, Secker & Warburg, 1999
4. Gilles Deleuze & Félix Guattari, *A Thousand Plateaus*, (tr. Brian Massumi), UMP, 1980.

with their own label. Information accounts for a world that is objectively determined (How might one account for something without determining it?). We understand why the language of information belongs to and is characteristic of the era of science and technology, thanks mostly to Husserl and Heidegger. 'Objective' language accounts for an equally 'objective' world. Modern science's great presumption is that everything is determinable, with a type of determination incompatible — being as it is of a different nature — with the indetermination produced by the uncertainty principle of quantum physics. The idea that determination is accompanied by the idea of power does not escape us: knowing how things are allows one to be more efficient when manipulating them. Information means, in a way, control and domination ('Information is — as the saying goes — Power'). It is a paradox: on the one hand the language of information determines and assures things, while on the other, the vast majority of information today is continuously reproduced before disappearing, substituted for ever newer information. They say that: 'Everything is Information', the world now being covered with underwater cables, rolled over by silent waves. Fluxes and dense packets of information at optical velocities. In this new environment, we either sink or swim. Or both.

Even though philosophy has rejected research into the perfect language, language of information along with that of the scientific (or, more appropriately, scientistic) now seems to auto-constitute the paradigmatic model of language as they are the ones that explain the world. You see here the paradox: we are unable to control the world through maternal language and so, for some reason, we aim to do so through informative and scientistic language. Why? We orientate ourselves through colloquial language, while we aim to control through informative language. Why is natural language more modest than the other? What manner of relationship with the world does each represent? We 'obtain' information. We don't obtain the meaning of things.

Judgement and common sense require maturity; and it is not the same to obtain information as it is to have good sense. And this woe has reached the so-called human and social sciences. Those who exhibit studies, while perhaps unknowingly, have only a simulation of language, not one thing or the other: it has neither different layers nor the flexibility of natural language, nor the rigour of formal language and the physical sciences. As such, at this point, the scandal moves towards the ridiculous. There is no maturity of judgement and the intended dominium of the object with its own, specialised language is an illusion. They are simulations that, hide on the one hand mediocrity, while on the other, cultural disorientation.

Though not all is lost. Information contains the notion of formation and with this, the need for a figure, consistency, form… Were it to play the opposite role of dispersion, it would be enough if some once again possessed information moving towards formation of the person, even only marginally. This way, the essence would be allowed to resonate. But that which instructs is not an accumulation, but rather quality over quantity. The professor teaching their students, parents educating their children, the spiritual leader caring about those close to them, etc.; all have to preoccupy themselves with the gesture, the word, the look that instructs. Though today it is intensifying, that which we lose is ever the same, just as this invaluable anecdote from the Desert Fathers shows us. It is said that the Abba Theodore refused to say anything to a brother who went to see him and that when one of his followers recriminated him for it, he replied: 'I did not speak to him, for he is a trafficker who seeks to glorify himself through the words of others'. It is not difficult to imagine the scene; we see similar ones everywhere and lists of these kinds of words are unending — mostly because beneath the label of 'innovation' there is a strange craving to back them up.

Sometimes, what is most important is to be found in ruins, and even where the vestiges of the essence have been erased. The squandering of language and its degradation have distinct forms, and both chattering and muttering play their parts. Verbal diarrhoea — defined as talking excessively — is linked to chattering in the sense that excess means a lack of substance. To a certain extent, current society has evolved from propaganda to chattering (whilst maintaining the former). And just as there is both more explicit and more subtle, hidden propaganda, there is chattering of the crude, scandalous type, as well as that which is dressed up in science and seriousness.

Muttering consists of speaking in a low voice, especially when complaining about something or saying bad things about people. Murmurs and background noise. Here, Saint Benedict's reflections are most wise. Surprisingly, muttering was one of the things that most worried Benedict, naturally appearing in his work many times. For example: 'Most importantly, that the evil of muttering not manifest itself for any reason, whatever it is, not even in the smallest word or movement.'[5] And he provokes a smile with this next excerpt in which he links the problem of wine with that of muttering:

'Even while we read that wine belongs in no way to monks, with everything, just as in these our times we are unable to make it understood, at least we don't tend to drink excessively, but rather in moderation, as 'wine abandons even the wise'. So, if the conditions of the place mean that the quantity mentioned cannot be found, or much less, or none at all, then let them bless God all those who live there, and let them not mutter. Most importantly, we advise the following: that they avoid muttering.'[6]

5. Benedict of Nursia, *Rule of Saint Benedict*, (tr. translator's own)
6. *Ibid.*

These days, muttering doesn't come from a lack of wine; in fact, rather than a scarcity of anything, it comes from an excess of practically everything. These days, complaints and mutterings are everywhere constantly. In the welfare society people often complain because, primarily, we believe ourselves to be subjects with numerous rights. But, unlike the more transparent protest and complaint, muttering is half hidden, its timidness forming part of its baseness. It has not the courage for confrontation, being also closer to the other end of the spectrum when it comes to happiness and gratitude. As such, it is weak and sickly. Egocentric by definition, those who mutter nurture a sentiment of dissatisfaction and avarice before all in their immediate proximity. Because of this, it sickens and weakens both the body and spirit through the bitterness its dissatisfaction contains. It has nothing to do with compassion or with the denunciation of injustice. What role does language play here? When muttering, language deteriorates until the words no longer have meaning. All that is left is the monotony of undifferentiated phenomes. The monotone tells you everything you need to know. Were only the tone, and no words, to remain, nothing would be lost and, in its context, the action would achieve the same function. As such, muttering is the perfect example of the empty word, of treachery of the word and is its cheap imitation. Words have power over life and death, but muttering has only the power of the worm eating away at its world. It projects nothing, nor is it capable of anything. It does but rot.

If Saint Benedict is quick on the perverse effects of muttering, then in his later pieces of writing, Foucault defends *frankness* in a way that I find very significant and apt for that which we are currently discussing. It deals with the Greek concept of *parrhesia* that Foucault considers closely linked to the similarly classical topics of *care of the self* and *ascesi*. *Parrhesia* is frankness, placing everything in the word (though not saying just everything); it's sincerity, being whole when speaking. Etymologically, *parrhesia* means 'all utterance' or 'all speech': not in the sense of the whole or completeness, but rather in the intention of saying that which one thinks. It is in contrast to demagogy and rhetoric, both of which aim only to persuade. Wishing not to excel, it simply aims to say that which is thought. While rhetoric is long, embellished discourse, *parrhesia* is dialogue and the 'face to face'. Being frank and sincere often requires courage. It is also often easier to pretend. The *parrhesiastes* is ever in a situation of convenient inferiority in terms of the person they are addressing, ever from lower down (like Socrates addressing the assembly). *Parrhesia* is the condition of a real, true relationship with the other (without rhetoric or adulation). In the care of the self, the word is of capital importance. Could it be anything but a sincere word? It refers to those who speak frankly, speak freely, and this is why the translation of *parrhesia* into Latin is *libertas*. To speak with liberty is to transform the self. There is a connection between the *parrhesia* of which Foucault speaks, the austerity of words of the Fathers of the Desert, and Saint Benedict's precaution when faced with muttering.

Muttering and demagogy are poison for the whole community. And there are ingenious quantities of it throughout society, from day-to-day life, through the mass media, reaching all the way into politics and culture and academia. It is miserable, empty, uninterrupted speech that contains and provides nothing.

What's more, deeply opposite to the essence: trickery, insults, and violence. The violence is mute, even when it can be accompanied by words; it being of the order of indifference. Worse than error is trickery, and worse than trickery are insults. As such, the insult is much further from the essence than error; and because of this, the essence of language has a lot more to do with sincerity than with truth. Vicious language is like the cut of a knife; a 'viper's tongue', as poisonous as that of the adder. Vicious language not only injures and kills others, but also the self.

Here you have, in what is but a quick summary, the different forms and grades of the squandering of language, of the distancing from the essence and even the treachery of the word.

SILENCE SO AS TO REDEEM THE WORD

Silence, on the other hand, is not mute, but often very significative and eloquent. The opposite of the word is not silence but — as we have just said — violence. Yet this phenomenon is often misunderstood as death is also silence, and after the bombs have been dropped, silence reigns across the battlefields. There are, therefore, very different forms of silence. One of them is undoubtedly the best cure for the degenerative illnesses of the word; distance from the maelstrom and access to the essence. For example, solitude and silence are indispensable conditions for all manner of religious life in particular and, in general, all manner of minimally consistent life. Why is silence the best place for prayer and petition? Why is silence the word's fertile womb? Is it because it is the required condition for listening and proximity? The largest rivers — like the most magnanimous people — are the most silent. Silence is, in effect, an exercise of a way out and access. Of going out from that which encloses and access to serenity and calm. Of going out from the noise and hackneyed, insignificant news, and access to crumbs of excellence. Of going out from binding canopies, acceleration, and ambient noise (the musical thread of the seventies and eighties that has been substituted by the uninterrupted information of the modern world) and access to the open plain. As Goethe said; 'Over all the hills now, repose'. And all repose is a hill: there where one might hear once again the hum of the essence. There is a passage from the Book of Job that has always fascinated me. When Job's friends get wind of the calamities that have happened to him, they go to see him: 'Then they sat on the ground with him for seven days and seven nights. No one said a word to him, because they saw how great his suffering was'.[7] This silence, accompanying and consoling, is the primordial word. And yet, this passage is afterwards overshadowed by the many conversations had between the three friends. Most certainly, they talk too much; it would have been better had they saved their words and focussed, instead of their unbridled discourse, on what can be found in silence.

At times we say: 'Can you hear the silence?' How can we *hear* silence? And what is this *hearing* of silence that enters us, allowing us to hear it?

TACTFUL CONTACT (OR LEVINAS' 'SAYING')

Levinas has made it even more obvious that the 'primordial language' or the *logos* of the prologue (pre-*logos*) is proximity and contact. Quite exquisitely he shows us how both the *Saying* and the *caress* are forms of proximity. Both are the expression of a responsibility that surpasses any reciprocal relationship. That the other is a sibling means this: that I am linked to this person through requirement and request. And that insomnia (the very definition of our psychism) is the situation in which the other places me. What is the difference between the *Said* (*le dit*) and the *Saying* (*le dire*)? According to Levinas, the *Said* is language destined to formulate that which is: to represent the world, to order it and, therefore, to understand it. In contrast, the *Saying* corresponds to an 'occurrence of proximity'[8] and is the 'primordial language'. The *Saying* signifies a responsibility without sentences or words and comes before verbal language: it is a 'prologue to languages'. The *Said* is language of categorisation; it deals with bringing things into focus and somehow constructing them or,

7. Job 2:13, New Revised Standard Version
8. The Levinas quotes are from a text called '*Langage et proximité*' [*Language and Proximity*] from: Emmanuel Levinas, *En Découvrant l'Existence avec Husserl et Heidegger* [*Discovering Existence with Husserl and Heidegger*], (tr. translator's own)

in Husserlian terminology, giving them meaning, fixing them, identifying them as what they are (the hammer as a hammer), saying them. Language as the *Said* recounts the world. Identification is the basis of categorisation: of converting something into a category. But this priority of identification allows Levinas to affirm that there is some kind of priority of the universal (and the idealistic) in respect to the singular. And, still within this register, communication is subsidiary, basically consisting of the transmission of messages. In contrast to this, Levinas' thesis is that: 'Regardless of the message transmitted through discourse, speech is contact', meaning that the same discourse is due to a singularity that is not categorised by the discourse, but rather only approached. And that 'the proximity is *for itself* significance'. This meaning, previous to that of categorisation, is — according to Levinas — the *primordial language*, the foundation of the other. I identify things and I pronounce them, and I say them to the other, who I don't identify, but to whom I approach. What happens, however, is that this approximation goes before and is more basic than the identification and is the first sense of language; the 'identification' and discourse come after. It is proximity, also called *ethical relationship*. In a footnote, Levinas defines it as such:

We call a relationship ethical when it is between two subjects, neither of which is united by a synthesis of understanding or by the relationship between subject and object but that in which one carries more weight or is more important or significant than the other, yet they are united by an intrigue that knowledge is not able to exhaust or unravel.

Proximity has nothing to do with increasing the microscope. Levinas deals with the dimension of sensibility which, in turn, manifests itself best through touch (not sight): 'Though sensibility must primordially be interpreted as touch'. The taste of things and the touch of the skin. In general, we have placed too much importance on sight: on the distant gaze, collective vision, contemplation, etc. But vision itself could be interpreted in terms of touch: 'One sees and listens as one touches,' says Levinas. The 'attentive gaze' — of which I have spoken before — seeks to, in part, interpret the look as touch, understanding it as an act of approximation through touch.

In this adventure, the caress becomes revelatory: 'It is the unit of both approximation and of proximity'. But proximity, being the presence of our faces, our skin, is also absence. In proximity there is the trace of the infinite (and perhaps, therefore, it's important to use the word 'trace' rather than 'footprint', as a footprint is a sign left in the earth by a human or animal; a trace is simply a sign left in passing by someone or something). The caress cannot be possession; it is proximity without identification or possession. It belongs to the family of *Saying*.

Saying is unconnected to power and is at the very heart of anarchy. In fact, the *Saying* is the expression of anarchy, of a situation in which the asymmetry has nothing to do with control, but rather with welcome and reception. Persuasive rhetoric is in the service of power. The anarchic *Saying* is not concerned with securing discursive milestones: it doesn't insist on the 'it's that *I have said* that...' All importance rests in the *Saying*, while the *Said* is relegated to second place.

Finally, in summary, we agree with Levinas that: 'Perhaps we have stopped admiring ourselves for all of the implications of proximity and approximation.'[9] And it's due to this that we are confused in terms of what the essence of speech does, our attention diverted to some place it shouldn't be. This, unlike Heidegger, allows Levinas to evaluate daily language: 'In day-to-day language we approach the fellow being instead of forgetting him in the "enthusiasm" of eloquence.'[10] This is, in effect, the role

9. Emmanuel Levinas, *Autrement qu'être ou au-delà de l'essence* [Otherwise than Being, or Beyond Essence], (tr. translator's own), 1974
10. Emmanuel Levinas, *Hors sujet*, [*Off Topic*], (tr. translator's own) Fata Morgana, 1987.

of the apparently insignificant conversation: talking about the weather, football or work is a way of approximating oneself to the other. The subject matter is secondary, and what is important is to respond to the relationship. At times, if the conversation is with someone we don't know, then we 'break the ice' and respond to the first contact, it being the first demand. It is unnecessary to remember that degeneration is ever easy, and that loose tongues and rumours invade our daily lives.

Language as non-indifference before the other; non-indifference vaccinated before the solicitations of eloquence; non-indifference far from knowledge and power; non-indifference that comes from proximity and that, at the same time, signifies a transcendence. This here is Levinas. While, in his later pieces of work, he masterfully pulls on this thread until speaking of the condition of *hostage* and *substitute*, here we read the pre-*logos* as both petition and protection.

THE ARCH-GESTURE

We accept that, as the overwhelming interpretation of language is that of information and communicative exchange, placing its essence in the notion of protection is somewhat surprising. What might help us to reduce this surprise is to look at how some primordial words reflect primordial gestures. For example, *no* is not the *no* of negation, but rather the *no* in the face of pain and suffering; *no* as rejection, as a barrier and a refusal of that which is presented as injury or threat, like two open hands placed in front of a body eager to avoid any trouble. Little separates this *no* from petition; unable to avoid the inevitable, language turns to pleas and exclamation. *Yes*, on the other hand, is said with a relaxed face and shining eyes; that which is expressed in the greetings of the Franciscans: 'Peace and All Good'. *Peace* and *Good* are not abstract concepts but rather the expression that alludes to the mother's words — lovingly whispered — with which she wraps up and protects the baby; the friend's silent, ubiquitous, welcoming word; the word of the teacher: for how can one teach without welcoming?

I repeat: the word is not the house of the being, but the house of the *human* being. It protects, swathes and comforts; it acts as a blanket, the text like material — if good, then it caresses and protects the skin.

'How are you?', 'How are you feeling?', 'It's good to see you', 'Take care', 'Goodbye', etc. are all expressions of shelter and welcome. In paying closer attention to them, can we not marvel in their meaning? 'Are you well?' is caring for the other. Literally speaking, it is a question, but in reality, it is touch and the joining of hands. The hand that caresses the child feels its body, its heartbeat. But it also instils warmth; you see how they are while also having a bearing on them. If 'How are you?' was always asked frankly, then egoism and indifference would recoil in the face of kindness just as verbal diarrhoea would recoil before the word.

As the arch-gesture has an ethical rather than declarative function, repetition makes complete sense. In effect, repetition of the question: 'Are you ok?' should not seem strange to anyone. The demand for care and shelter is ever present. As such, repetition of the welcome makes a lot more sense than the repetition of declarations. The effects of the word, a gift of the present, are extended into the past and the future. Temporal dilation and the diachrony of protection. One can speak of those no longer with us or of the tomorrow that will be. It is a word that intensifies the resources of consolation and discovers more avenues for calm and confidence. If not, why would we miss the caressing, cordially resonating word so much?

At times, even when language seems only to 'inform of the fact', it is doing something quite distinct: someone is addressing someone else to tell them about something that has happened or that they see and it's as if they were placing 'the facts' in the palm of their hand and raising it slowly up in an offering to the other. Then, becoming aware of the facts would be subordinate to my relationship with the other, who I address solicitously. We welcome by explaining the world: 'Look how the day is, look at the green grass, look at the train…'

We have now exchanged Heidegger's *dictum* of 'language is the house of the being' for the idea that the word — of the other — is the house of the human (and, as such, also of the being). Here is the idea that runs through Cormac McCarthy's *The Road*: in the midst of the devastation and cruelty, all that is left is the love and shelter provided by the father for his son, and by the son for his father. But the extreme harshness of the situation leads to petition, defences, and shelter. One asks and petitions because of the precariousness of the situation. Mostly, though, it is for others that things are asked.

The human being itself is a petition and, as Rosenzweig says on one of his more memorable pages, language has the power of petition:

'To petition is the most human act of all. Even man's silence can petition. And it is there that natural muteness seems to triumph over the tongues of men, dealing with the language of petition. The mute eye of the animal can petition. Through petition does the human awaken in human. The petition is the child's first word. And at the same time, it is the first word of those who awaken from the dream of infancy.'[11]

But there is no need to run to thinkers linked to Jewish or Christian dialogical thought to put this into perspective. George Bataille's reflections when describing the interior experience are revelatory:

'State of nudity, of supplication without response, wherein I nevertheless

11. Franz Rosenzweig, *Das Büchlein vom gesunden und kranken Menschenverstand* [*Understanding the Sick and the Healthy: A View of World, Man, and God*], (tr. translator's own)

perceive this: that it depends on the flight from excuses. So that — precise knowledge remaining as such, with only the ground, its foundation, giving way — I grasp while sinking that the sole truth of man, glimpsed at last, is to be a supplication without response.'[12]

A petition without response. And here you see how he alludes to the calming function of the words:

My eyes are open, it is true, but it would have been necessary not to say it, to remain frozen like an animal. I wanted to speak and, as if the words bore the weight of a thousand slumbers, gently, as if appearing not to see, my eyes closed.

Calming, sleep inducing words, thinks Bataille. Fine. But why is there no mention of anybody else? Why is it that in his pages, Bataille doesn't consider the other, when precariousness emerges, especially in the other. Where is the solicitation, the care, the love for the other? Petition and plea are, as Antoine de Saint-Exupéry says, connected to love: 'Love is, first and foremost, an exercise of petition, and petition is an exercise of silence'.

Petition, prayer, already effective, at the margins of the result: it reduces but a little the desperation and serves as judgement; it is interior life, reflection, meditation. Petition, prayer, in which the speaker manifests themself more than the receiver. When there is calm, it's as if prayer maintains the world. It rises up, takes off and opens the doors to the heavens. And it is then that the heavens become, at least for a while, serene.

The most profound spirit of philosophy resembles the petition in the sense that in both cases it is deprived of responses. And it's because of this that there exists a philosophy that is (like) a petition, and that many petitions are, for their part, the most genuinely unsettling expression of philosophy. And so that which counts the most, much more than any other possible

12. Georges Bataille, *Inner Experience*, (tr. L.A. Boldt), SUNYP, 1988

attributes, is the sincerity without which petition is clearly not petition. Philosophical petition doesn't demand any explanation, rather meaning; it asks not for a system, but rather a path; it asks not for greatness, but breadcrumbs; it confirms not, rather asking and waiting.

In various ways, Feuerbach, Marx, Nietzsche and Freud have insisted that the idea of God is a projection not only created *by* us, but also *of* us. Feuerbach, while starting out a Hegelian, proceeded to the reversal of ideas that Marx would later inherit. 'The true statement is this: man's knowledge of God is man's knowledge of himself, of his own nature.'[13] Here is the theology's reduction to anthropology that has lasted up until modern times with enormous, far-reaching impact. This is Feuerbach's thesis: 'Man is the revealed God: in man the divine essence first realises and unfolds itself'. God is an illusion, a mirror in which man sees man. God has been made in the image of man.' Clearly, Feuerbach has the God of the Gospels in mind. So then, is this argument refutable, as has been attempted so many times from 'positions of belief'? Rather the contrary: it seems to me that what is required is its radicalisation. Then something unexpected happens: it is not that the argument changes direction, but that it clearly exceeds what Feuerbach had originally proposed. And is this radicalisation not that which we have been discussing with the arch-gesture, the essence of the word? Instead of speaking about 'projection' — *a la* Feuerbach — we would rather opt for 'familiarity' or 'communion' in the essence of speech, of which the connotation is different. Familiarity doesn't mean a lack of *transcendence*, it sooner implicates it. To think of transcendence is to think of the difference in terms of the hope in the gesture itself.

13. Ludwig Feuerbach, *The Essence of Christianity*, (tr. M. Evans), Trüber & Co., 1881

Masters of sharpness. In a letter to Hugo Boxel, Spinoza wrote that a speaking triangle would say that God is triangular. Two and half centuries later, Franz Rosenzweig retorted that: 'The triangle, if it could speak, would say that God speaks.'[14]

But how would God speak? Without doubt, the greatest desire would be that he or she spoke according to the essence of human speech; that God spoke not so much to gossip or to explain how the world and its rules are, but rather in terms of protection and shelter, the arch-gesture of the human word. In times past, people would also once say: 'God protect you!' The word of God is shelter, and shelter is God.

To guard means both to watch attentively and to care for. To protect is to pay attention, care for, respect, to watch over something so that it isn't hurt. *To protect, to watch over* and *to shelter* express the fundamental notion of our being. We protect so as to shelter, to watch over, to keep from harm and from disappearance, just as one keeps a memory. And memory is one of the most privileged ways of caring. 'Take away memory, and love vanishes', wrote Rousseau; protect and watch over the word of the memory (the cordial word) and protect and watch over the word of the promise. 'The simplest words' — writes Emerson — 'we do not know what they mean except when we love and aspire.'[15]

We can imagine ourselves naming everything in the universe (and having theories for it all), and yet experiencing the same tininess and helplessness, lessened only by the friendly word that doesn't exhibit the truth of things, but that transmits the embrace of the spirit.

14. Franz Rosenzweig, *Der Mensch und sein Werk* [*Man and his Work*], (tr. translator's own)
15. Ralph Waldo Emerson, *Emerson's Essays*, Harper, 1951. This is equivalent to Saint Paul's words: 'If I speak in the tongues of mortals and of angels, but do not have love, I am a noisy gong or a clanging cymbal.' (Corinthians 13:1, New Revised Standard Version).

X. A METAPHYSICS OF CONJUNCTION

No need for it to be definitive or to explain it all in depth; it is certainly not within our reach. But we can make do with a clue, even a discreet one, so as to talk about human existence. It has been left behind in the traditional blueprint of an essence that, furthermore, used to exist (that's to say, of an essence that used to be 'in act'). The concept of existence, especially after Kierkegaard and Heidegger, is now different: it has gone from being a realisation of an essence to indicating our exclusive *way of being*. Indeed, strictly speaking, only humans exist. It is a way of being that manifests itself as both a movement of going out and of 'reflection'. In other words, it is autoreferential, folding in on itself. It is a part of the movement of existence. Even though one can talk of maturity, existence doesn't have as much to do with milestones accomplished and achievements as tension and vigilance. Existence as pensive tension seeks to protect and shelter the self and others, all the while desiring more comprehension. Care, solicitude and shelter are all linked to the experience of finitude and vulnerability, also to the same experience, partial clarity, light and knowledge. Which clue might help us to understand ourselves a little better?

As if we were a joint, a stitch, a provisional seam between two points. Death is the unravelling or breaking of the thread, of the stitch. Until then, temporality is shown as a precarious, vulnerable cosmicity. Because of this, it makes sense to care for both ourselves and others. Life's mythical thread is not the cord linking us to totality, but rather each specific part that sews two points together and, as such, makes way for each and every singular, unrepeatable life. We are a connection, a *gathering*, a *conjunction*, as precarious as it is admirable. A meeting of differences. The conjunction supposes, in effect, a connection of that which is different and, as such, is neither homogeneity nor transparency. This is why we ask ourselves who we are. Our identity — as Ricoeur would say — implies alterity: oneself as much as the other; our identity as the deepest self, an ipse identity, implying alterity, difference, and tension.

The figure of conjunction allows us to recover some already well-known distinctions, transforming them. For example, while we now find the language of the old dualisms unacceptable, the underlying experience cannot be underestimated. There are also some types of ascendant language applied to knowledge and spiritual life that at times we find a little old-fashioned. Nevertheless, there is a characteristic *tension* present in both intellectual and moral life that we must know how to express once more.

A joint or provisional stitch between two points. Conjunction. What does it mean to 'do metaphysics' on this idea? Well, not to see if it takes us further away, but if it brings us back here, back to foundations, to the sinus of existence. Metaphysics, therefore, is an act of hermeneutics on the conjunction.

Unexpectedly, today metaphysical discourse has not only a polemical, but also a liberating, meaning. We are so worn out by scientific explanations about the human being that it is more than ever in our interests to focus on another level of depth, that is not incompatible with what there already is, but rather distinct and, most importantly, more radical. The philosophical mission is to avoid reductionism. If this is achieved, then its role within the community is more than justified. Metaphysics today consists of focussing on the constitutive experiences of the human situation and, in doing so, investigating a register that is more fundamental than that in which various scientific specialities move. As such, it is important not to confuse plans or levels of radicality. It is not in our interests to look for an explanation of irreversibility or vulnerability in neuroscience. The metaphysics we are aiming for is not, therefore, a direct access to another world, but rather an interpretation of the human situation and the movement of existence. Another thing — something for another day — is whether this same movement represents some kind of rift within the world.

HUMAN SITUATION, NEIGHBOURING ZONE

In order to understand this idea of conjunction, let's take a brief detour. As we have previously mentioned, the subject of limits has often been dealt with in terms of an insurmountable doorstep: we cannot go further than *certain limits*. Another thing, however, is that the human *is* the limit. In order to understand the meaning of the word *limit* here, one must first revise the concept of 'limit situations' (*Grenzsituationen*) from the philosophy of Karl Jaspers. What is often quoted about this theory is its plural, in the sense that there are a number of limit situations. The intuitive idea is that it deals with bad, unsettling, difficult, or irresolvable situations. While some of these limit situations can happen sporadically, they are, in general, permanent and inevitable: 'I must die, I must suffer, I must struggle, I am subject to chance, I involve myself inexorably in guilt.'[1] According to Jaspers, these are the limit situations. In normal life — in the 'empirical existence' of the author's own terminology — we aim to avoid the limit situation and, when it comes a-knocking, leads to desperation and evasion — if possible — or also to confrontation, by placing oneself within the orientation of the *existence* described here: 'To experience the limit situations and exist are one and the same.'[2] He himself explains: 'We become ourselves by going into limit situations with our eyes wide open.'[3] It is no coincidence that, while he explains little, Jaspers' reflection contains a reference to

1. Karl Jaspers, *Way to Wisdom*, (tr. R. Manheim), YUP, 1954
2. Karl Jaspers, *Philosophie II. Existenz-erhellung*, Springer, 1973 (tr. translator's own)
3. *Ibid.*

the *difference*: 'Empirical existence, like consciousness, is unable to conceive of the difference.' Empirical existence lies in homogeneity, in monochromatic life, while on the other hand, the limit situation leads to the emergence of the difference as it reveals an impenetrable depth of some limit. *Difference, limit* and the *prologue to transcendence* serve to indicate the same experience. The limit, while found in the heart of immanence, points towards transcendence. Experience of a limit situation can, along with doubt and admiration, be another source of philosophy. For Jaspers, there are situations that are not limit situations: they are, we would say, daily situations lacking much importance. And yet it turns out that, limit or not, *we are always in a situation.* And there is a moment in which Jaspers mentions — in passing — this 'always in a situation' as one of the limit situations.⁴ It is this idea that we adopt, bring back home and, once there, ask ourselves: 'How might we understand the human situation in such a way that it always includes the limit?' It is a question that aims to therefore dispense with the plural and leave to one side the distinction between a 'normal' situation and limit situations, rather considering that the *in a situation* — to exist — is always a limit situation because the *human situation* is a limit. As such, and in contrast with the first reading, what is important in the expression *limit situation* is the *situation* rather than the *limit*, as it is already included in it. What's more, we should add that the term *human situation* would be redundant, as the actual situation mentioned *is* the human situation. If at times we talk of *situating* a piece of furniture, it would be more appropriate to talk of *placing it* or *setting it*. The concept of *situation* can even be considered as belonging more to the human being than that of *condition*. Let us therefore repeat the question, while adding another: why does the concept of *situation* include the *limit*? And what concept of limit does it include?

The limit has often been understood as being at the limit, at

4. *Ibid.*

the extreme, on the edge of the precipice, under tension that is difficult to cope with: 'At the limit of my strength', for example. An unsustainable situation provoking a desperate desire for peace and calm. The limit has also been understood — as we have just shown — as 'the capacity to reach': the limit of my capacity for knowledge, the limit of my capacity to speak, the limit of my capacity to do. It's limit as limitation, as a doorstep that is impossible to overcome, as a barrier to going any further. What stands out in this sense are the limits of my body as an 'I can' and the limits of knowledge and language (the considerations of which have given way to negative theology and all of the different forms of philosophy that come with it).

But there is *another possibility*: to consider the limit as a *neighbouring zone* and demonstrate it as the most definitive thing of the *human situation*. The neighbouring zone is the stitched area, the seam, there where hooks bring together two points, without the most decisive being to name them: body and spirit, the heavens and the earth, time and eternity, the finite and the infinite, forever and never, horizontal and vertical, etc. The most decisive, in other words, is not to give names to the stitched together limits, but rather that the stitch and the difference it supposes is appropriate. The limit as a neighbouring zone becomes a key to interpretation that shows its fruitfulness as, instead of discarding, it allows us to continue with the relevant subjects under a new light. It is a concept-figure in which others are propagated and allows us to reinterpret the *opening* (the light and awareness), the notion of the *finite* (uncertainty and the end), the *foreign interior* (in line with Agustin, Ricoeur, and Heidegger), care for the bandages of the *other* (and language as shelter) and the *difference* (metaphysics as difference).

The reflection and refraction of light are related to neighbouring zones. In optics, reflection is explained as a change in the direction of a ray of light when it cannot pass through the interface between two objects. We transfer this physical explanation to a philosophical one so that the limit situation might account for the possibility of reflection (for which the condition requires a minimum amount of light). Heidegger had the fine idea of translating and reading the traditional subject of intellectual capacity, or natural light (*lumen naturale*) as an opening for *Dasein*. The opening of *Dasein* is its clearing; being open means that it is the 'place' in which things can manifest themselves. Opening, clearing, space for things to appear, light (auto-illumination and illumination of things). Heideggerian thought becomes complicated and difficult when it establishes its interpretation of this *being-with* (in other words, the human) as neighbourhood or proximity of the being itself. There is no need for us to follow this path: we will continue our lecture using the already mentioned terms. Reflection is flection on oneself. Consciousness (effectively, awareness) is understood as a reflection; a movement that flexes on itself, like when we bend a cane and point its tip back downwards. Light's great mystery is not that it illuminates everything, but that, by doing so, it also illuminates itself. Light illuminates and auto-illuminates. And so, consciousness and self-consciousness coincide. Yet reflection is neither absolute nor universal. There is a special, definitively privileged space in which it can be seen: the human situation. The mystery intensifies (or, in fact, constructs itself) because the reflection is but partial (will it ever be complete?), ever producing both light and darkness, presence and absence, apparitions and disappearances. We are this place of partial reflection; a clarity on itself, clarity on its own clarity, but only ever a semi-clarity. Is it not this that answers (the condition of possibility of) the last questions, among which there is the one that asks about that which does not appear, that slips away from the apparition, that is the *background to the world* (if it is that world that appears) and that, in fact, is the condition of the appearance itself? The possibility is that we are transfixed — essentially implicated — by the marvel of the light. If one wished, one might call it 'our relationship with the truth'. The conjunction as a neighbouring zone alludes to this implication.

WEAKNESS OF THE CONJUNCTION

An unfinished conjunction. Unfinished or, rather, finite and temporary. A seam: like the sewing together of long or wide points bringing together two pieces of cloth. A provisional stitch that will someday be stitched over again, or not. What often emerges from the experience of the provisional nature of the seam is a kind of undefined hope.

It is not that the human is a sum or temporary union of two elements. The human is the conjunction, a conjunction that cannot be read in terms of dialectics or overcoming; it is not the next step, nor a phase among phases. It is an imperfect conjunction, unfinished, finite, but one that overcomes this finite nature with an intention that emerges from the folds of its limits.

The weakness of the conjunction and the mystery of individuality. A paradoxical weakness of intimacy that we have understood in the opposite way to Deleuze. Life is not more life within the impersonal current, but in the precarious personal position (or hypostasis). It doesn't matter that life has to strip off and get weaker so as to be personal. Without doubt, the subject is not as strong as it is weak. Yet the posterior process of the weakening of the weakness does not lead to more personality, but rather its disappearance. Personal life is the temporariness of a weakness, of a conjunction, situated in the very heart of the immanence of the impersonal current, like a short pause.

The conjunction is this pause. Each of these conjunctions is a pause brought about by the homogeneous design of the being or nothingness. And *one* is not the indeterminate, but rather individuality and one's own personal name. The impersonal current of life is made *a personal life* through the bringing together of the heavens and the earth.

The weakness of the conjunction. We care for ourselves, we protect ourselves, we protect one and another. We also hurt each other, because everything is sewn together and there are those who somatise the weakness of the hiatus through violence (a way of escaping from finitude). Violence comes from dogmatism (false strength), and dogmatism, from the weakness of pain suffered.

Nothing comes before the conjunction. Uncertainty is primordial, and we know not if it is the beginning or the end. That it is primordial means that, unlike gnostic and certain idealistic positions, there is no 'fall'. There is no loss of original plenitude or strength. Nor are we an injury. We are a precarious, uncertain conjunction, understood as vulnerability. And, just like the fall, the injury comes after. Precariousness is the possibility of injury through accident, illness, violence, etc. The conjunction is creation, a start: a thread binds two elements together and, with this, reflection and vulnerability enter the world. In effect, if one wished to continue speaking about falling, this would consist of either the previously mentioned violence or some kind of petrification of the conjunction and the consequent indifference towards the solicitude and care for one's fellow being. It is a fall either as *violence* or *indifference*.

To resist is to make sure that this conjunction doesn't come undone. All of the registers of resistance we have alluded to are reconciled with the figure of the conjunction.

The 'meaning' of this conjunction is clarity and shelter, comprehension and compassion. We have focussed our attention on shelter because it is freed from the ballast that accompanies the subject of compassion and also because it sheds light on the fundamental meaning. Then appear the caricature-like features of the treatment that Nietzsche makes of compassion when, along with love, he assimilates them into possessive forms: 'When we see somebody suffer, we like to exploit this opportunity to take possession of him.'[5] Nietzschean discourse insists that weakness invites possession and rejection: 'What is life? Life — that is: continually shedding something that wants to die. Life — that is: being cruel and inexorable against everything about us that is growing old and weak.'[6] Do possession and rejection comprehend each other in terms of that which is most typical of the relationship with weakness? We consider it to be the opposite. Because of this, the first word is *shelter* (without possession). It is not about possessing, but rather sheltering. Luckily, Nietzsche is too good. He hits us with the scene at the start of Zarathustra's return: the tightrope walker in the village square suddenly falls to the ground where, seriously injured, he is at death's door. The people step back and move out the way, but Zarathustra kneels down next to him, consoles him, and tells him that he will bury him with his own hands. The poor tightrope walker dies, and Zarathustra carries him on his back until, at the break of dawn, he is able to leave him within a tree with a hole halfway up it. This way, the wolves won't be able to reach him. Then, and only then, does Zarathustra lie down on the ground and fall asleep, 'weary in body but with a calm soul.'

The meaning of human junction is conjunction: conjunction as shelter from vulnerability and conjunction as the intention — the effort — to understand. One thing *and* the other. Not only a common root, but two expressions of the same movement. It's because of this, despite the already recognised geniality, that we nevertheless insufficiently see the Heideggerian figure of *Dasein* as clearing, as it has nothing to do with vulnerability or, as such, with the meaning of shelter. Looking for any Heideggerian ethic

5. Friedrich Nietzsche, *The Gay Science*, (tr. W. Kaufman), Vintage Books, 1974
6. *Ibid.*

would be in vain.

The meaning of existence is to strive for clarity and shelter. *To be aware of the human is to be implicated in the stitching of the stitch.* The weakness of the other leads medicine and ethics to mean the same thing. Each of us is a stitch that demands others' attention. And there is a priority of the stitch that is the other in respect to the stitch that I am myself; not only because were it not like this, extreme situations of sacrifice would be inexplicable, but because there is also a more habitual giving of the self that would be impossible to explain.

At this point, not only is the Heideggerian gesture strange; Deleuze's interpretation of the face is equally surprising. To start off: how is *faciality* to be spoken of? How is it that the meaning of the face gets closer through abstraction? Which hidden, un-noticed connection is there in relation to the abstraction of traditional metaphysics? Why is the face understood in terms of surface and holes (a surface full of black holes)? Deleuze refers to the 'abstract machine of faciality', a machine that is seen as effective even in the mother's face as she breastfeeds her child. Why does Deleuze, following in Nietzsche's footsteps, see power in the face, while Levinas sees but weakness and vulnerability? The divergence comes from the kind and use of abstraction. It's obvious that both writers work specifically with the face: in one case, the face throws off its nakedness and becomes a surface while, in the other case, the nakedness is what each face signifies (though, clearly, some more than others), that which is taken as a primary meaning. Playing little with abstractions, common sense quickly tells us which of the two is right. Who, when standing in front of a child, sees nothing but a surface with two holes?

The caress, according to Deleuze, is also power, and the aim is to leave, move and free oneself of all points and holes. We already know that black holes consume everything. So, move away from them, then. Yet one's fellow being is no hole or dominating, tyrannical power, but rather a face, an expression of provisional conjunction. There is implication and attraction, not in the sense of a bottomless well, but in the responsibility and sweetness of company. The caress is not power but the touch of contact.

THE HUMAN CONJUNCTION

The human is the conjunction because it makes the join. It's our *way of being*. We connect, we unite, we gather. Our ontological characteristic consists of the fact that we exist in union, stitched together. We are an *and*. Both discourse and shelter are forms of connection. The conjunction with others comes from *eros*, moving through *philia*, before arriving at *agape*. Self-esteem, rather than pride, is the effort for the conjunction itself. What does it mean, this constant attempt to understand ourselves and others? And the other form of conjunction appears through dialogue, with thought following close behind. Are not the symbol and the word types of conjunction? 'What we cannot speak about we must pass over in silence', went — as is well-known — the last of the propositions (or pseudo-propositions) in *Tractatus*. However, the same Wittgenstein was far too keen to ignore that in this proposition was expressed a prescription that philosophy has violated and — at the very best — will violate inexorably again and again. Can philosophy be made to not speak of precisely that which is difficult to speak of, not to mention impossible? Is it not true that *philosophy has been this paradoxical essay of speaking about that which cannot be spoken? That of which it is almost impossible to speak, that is of what philosophy speaks.* As such, the attention paid to it is also symbolic. The symbol is a seam, a union of the finite and infinite, of the world and the *trans*-world, of worldliness and alterity. To speak is to unite that which we have in front of us, but also to unite the things in front of me with the things that are not in front of me. Because of this, to speak is to speak of that which cannot be spoken of.

At the same time, the poetic word, the poetic image, is a magnificent attempt at conjunction. With the poetic word *conjoining is sheltering* is made explicit. Words make the spirit flow. And the spirit is nothing but the name we use for the shelter. Without spirit, the word is not the word. And with the spirit, all words are but solace.

DIFFERENCE

Weakness and superficiality, skin. Augustine intuition has been naturally interpreted through the blueprint of depth: we must go to the deepest parts of ourselves to make out the veiled presence of the infinite. But the interpretation can be very different with the model of the conjunction. Not necessarily enough to invert it and make an apologia for superficiality against depth, but rather to indicate that superficiality is also profound. If we leave the subject that contrasts superficiality and depth, we find ourselves faced with the reward that there is no longer any place for even the 'deep people' (who denigrate the superficiality) or the free (who criticise the pretension of depth so as to rid themselves of all meaning, of all centre). If it is true that superficiality might be a synonym of banality, then it is also true that superficiality is linked to the appearance of things in the light and then, the game between the superficial and the profound gets richer and more dynamic. Instead of contrasting each other, they are mutually implied, even transforming one into the other. Skin is both superficial and profound at the same time. The human existence (the conjunction) doesn't go beyond the skin, but rather goes in the skin itself. Metaphysics, then, eager for depth, is attention to the surface. The conjunction is the place where that which is superficial becomes profound and that which is profound becomes superficial; a place where the mysterious tension of the neighbouring zone is palpable.

After the dominance of representation and objectivism, metaphysics has turned towards the limit that supposes the same situation of who exists as a protagonist of the metaphysical question and, with this, the abstraction gives way to thoughtful attention, and the science of *ens* as *ens* is substituted for hermeneutics of conjunction. Where does the need for meaning come from? Why do we resist the fact that it all might be absurd?

We already know that meaning is linked to movement and direction. We understand the *meaning* of a plant's movement in the unfolding of its leaves in the sun and the sinking of its roots into the earth. The philosophical problem is not that of the being, but rather that of the meaning of the being. Part of contemporary philosophy is an effort to think of the meaning of the being (the meaning of the being as *unconcealment* in Heidegger, as *dwindling* and nihilation in Vattimo, as *beyond* the essence in Levinas, etc.).

We have explained why the meaning of human existence can in no way be unconnected to the nihilistic experience, an experience that can never be overcome and a shadow of that which is inevitable. It is the primordial trauma, despite being biographically preceded by a time yearned for by innocence. As such, existence is always post-traumatic. And so here it takes on all of its *meaning* in the *return to normality*, *distraction* or even *mourning*. The return to normality is that which we have contemplated as a task of making the day to day our own; distraction, ever partial, as a pause in a sentence; and mourning (as a task of the acceptance of loss) so as not to lose ourselves in loss and to resist in spite of everything.

We have also explained that willingness of comprehension and shelter is an expression of the same movement as resistance, of the meaning of resistance. But we note how this meaning *differs* from itself, it pushes us further than itself. As if it were partially postponed or delayed; as if its full significance were put off for later; as if an ulterior *co-conjunction* had demonstrated the complete meaning of the primary resistance (in the same way that the second time makes the first time, the first). The intimate resistance reveals itself as a meaning of life, though the meaning of this meaning differs from itself.

One's fellow being, the home, the day to day, care. These are all elements of a philosophy of proximity that recognises the nihilistic experience and exposure to helplessness as founding principles. These elements of proximity allow themselves to be integrated in the meaning of resistance. Common people have always known that resistance is worth it. Philosophical thought gets there late, but it gets there. That which moves it, though, cannot satisfactorily stop it there. It inevitably interrogates itself for a deferred meaning to this resistance. It glimpses that resistance makes even more sense than it first seems; there it glimpses a strange confidence. And so, it recognises that it — philosophical thought — has always formed part of this resistance, thus discovering that interrogation is also petition.